I0755706

Published in the United States by The Spiritual Highway Publishing

'

Edited by Angela Rose

Co-authored by Jennifer Bailey

Interior Layout and Cover Design by Jeffrey Ringer

Printed and bound in the United States

Published by

The Spiritual Highway Publishing

543 Country Club Dr. #B429

Simi Valley, CA 93065

818.671.5448

www.TheSpiritualHighway.com

Foreword

A couple of years ago, I was inspired to document my contemplative journey through photography. I sat down and began to write what each photo meant to me as I saw the image in my mind and through the lens of my camera. I feel so much in all that I see, loving the beauty that surrounds me even in the smallest things. However, it is a challenge to put my thoughts into words, as I am a much more visual person.

So the journey began. Filled with excitement, I composed the first half of this book in a few months. Then it sat untouched for the better part of a year while I tried to edit what I had written. I asked for help with the editing and received several suggestions and thoughts along the way. This was a huge transitional period in my life, in which I ended a marriage of 24 years, transitioned my career and took responsibility for where I am today.

Last year, I met the wonderfully inspiring and spiritual woman who helped me produce the work before you. Jennifer Bailey is a gifted spiritual coach and has been on amazing journey of her own. Together, we perfected the prose I had previously written, and as the book progressed, we added more of her energy and inspiration. I am truly grateful to have had her help and love.

In loving memory of my father, Marvin Arthur Cohen,
my creatively inspiring grandmother, Marian Levin,
and my grandparents, who always believed in me, Vic and Katie Ringer.

Dedicated to my two beautiful and gifted children, Matthew and Aryanna.

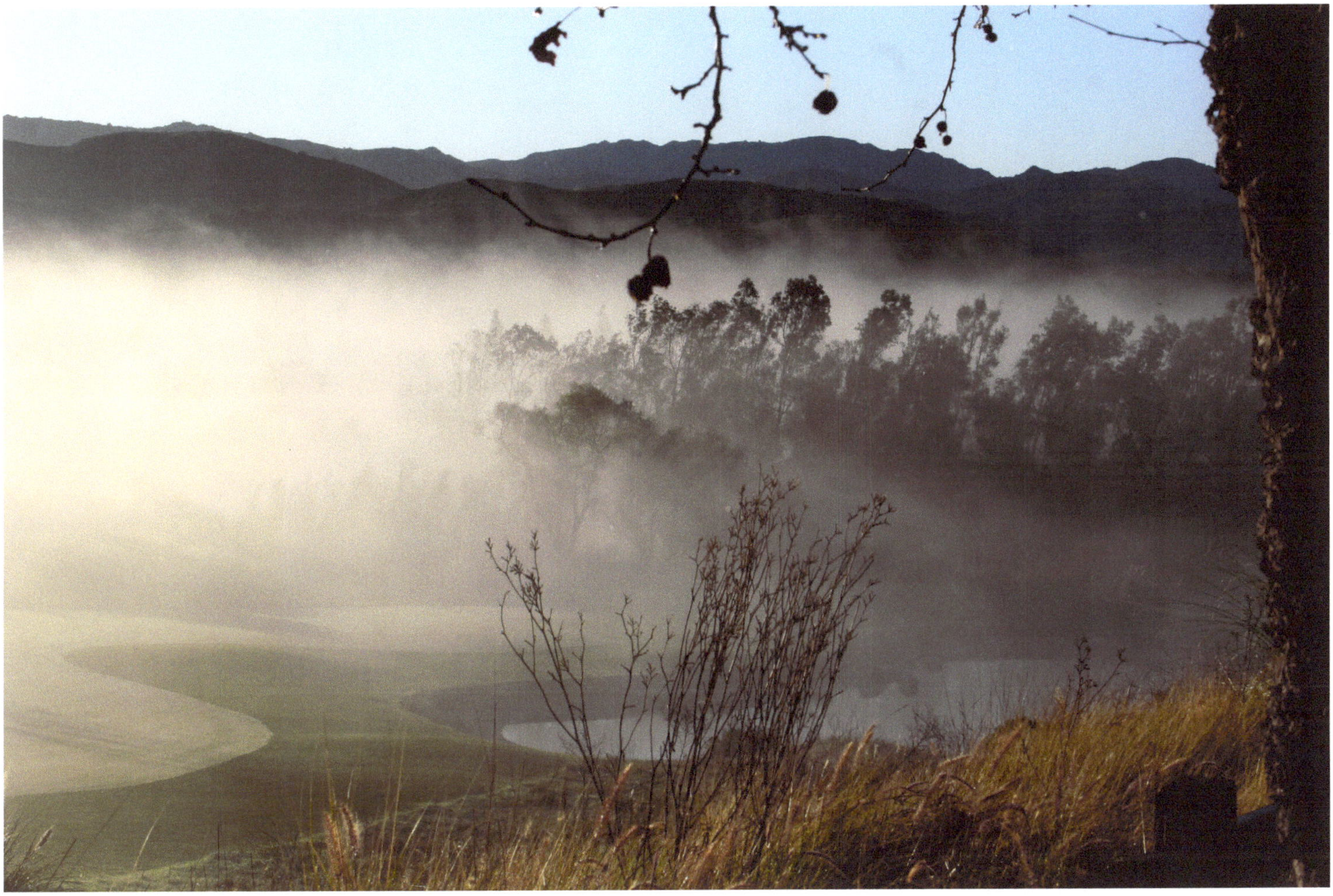

As I embarked on my daily journey,
I stopped to breathe in the beauty:

the fog hanging over the golf course,
the morning sun breaking through,
the long shadows and light streaming
across the lush green grass,
the putting green and the pond,
framed so elegantly by the trees.

Amid dangling branches and tall plants,
it was one of those magical moments.

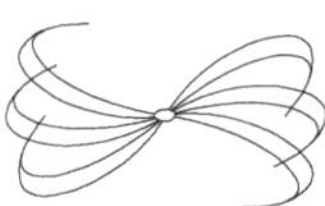

Meditation: Find a place to sit outside where you can appreciate the scenery. Breathe in the fresh air. How does it feel? Turn your attention to the scenery and look around. Breathe in the beauty. Notice the tiny details and marvel at how they all combine to form something larger than the whole.

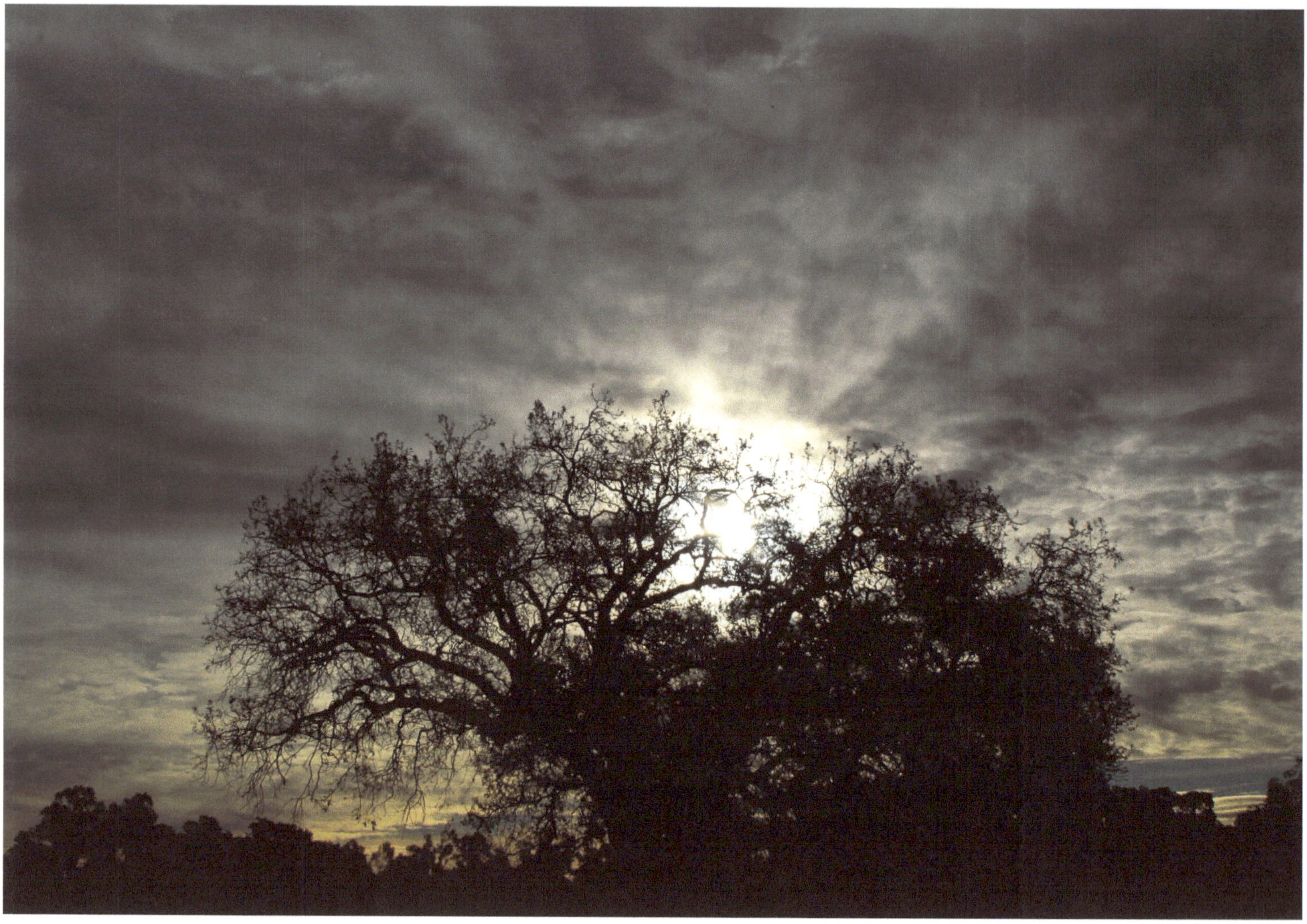

As far back as I can remember,

I have always loved the play between nature's elements.

The sun peeking through the clouds and trees,

creating breathtaking vistas

as they illuminate or obscure each other

in a natural game of hide and seek.

At nighttime, I love the way the moon

lights up the clouds and hides behind them.

Loving awareness leads to an enriched life.

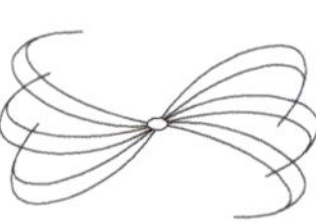

Meditation: On a cloudy day, or even a day with just a few wispy clouds, look to the sky and notice the interplay of clouds and light. Be mindful of any emotions that surface. Maybe there is a hidden message in their depths. Perhaps they share a sense of peace. Allow the white light shining through to be there for your protection.

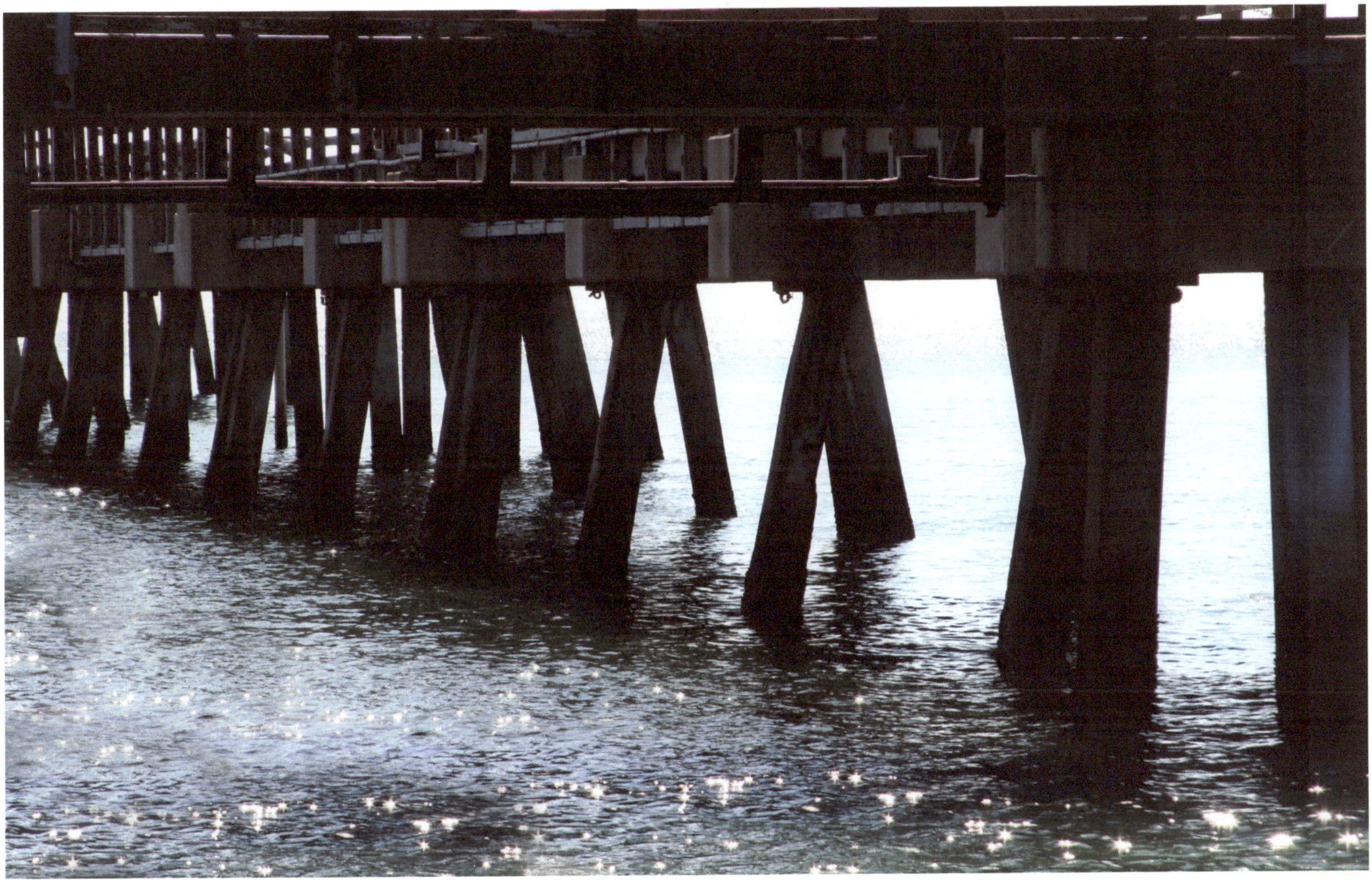

The light dances on the water,
playfully riding the tides
created by the gentle breeze.

The strength of the mighty pier,
standing tall
as the water washes against its sturdy pillars.

A parallel to the ebb and flow of life
with grand lessons, gifts,
and beautiful opportunities to grow.

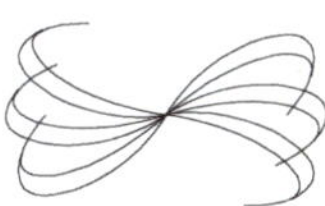

Meditation: The element of water is healing. Find a place to sit quietly, surrounded by the sound of flowing water. (Near an ocean, stream or fountain would be ideal.) In this moment, relax into a sacred place—a serene place of knowing within you. Remember, everything that comes into your life is here to teach you, evolve your soul and help you grow.

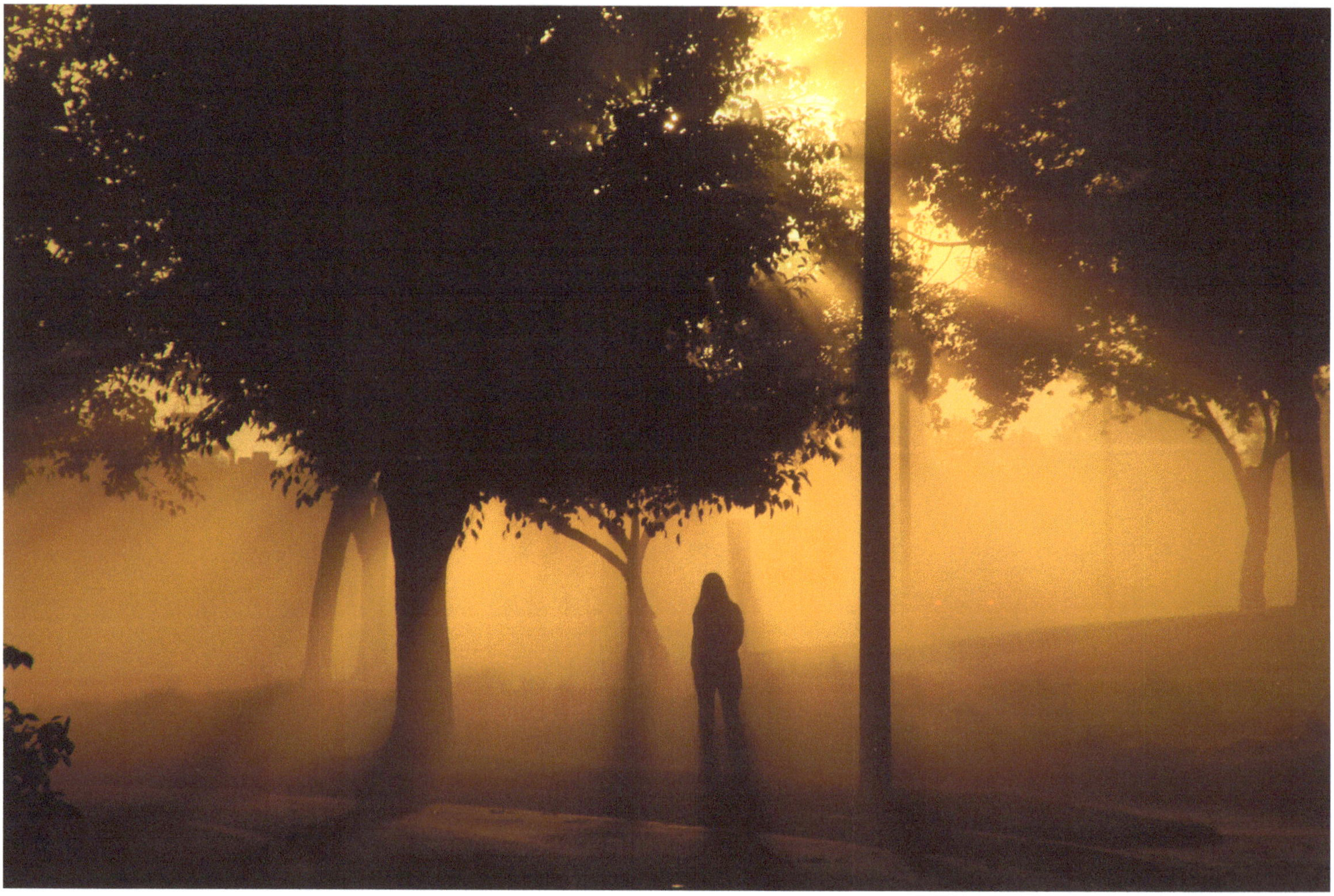

Early one morning,
the fog rolled in and grew very dense.
Magically, the golden sun began streaming through.
The shadows and highlights were irresistible.
At that moment, a woman appeared
and completed the scene.

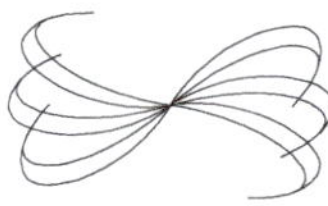

Meditation: Find a comfortable place to sit and begin observing your breath. Inhale and exhale for a few moments. When your mind begins to wander, gently bring yourself back to your breath. In your stillness, you will discover peace and freedom from mindless chatter and distractions. Breathe in calm, breathe out stress, and feel your body melt into total relaxation.

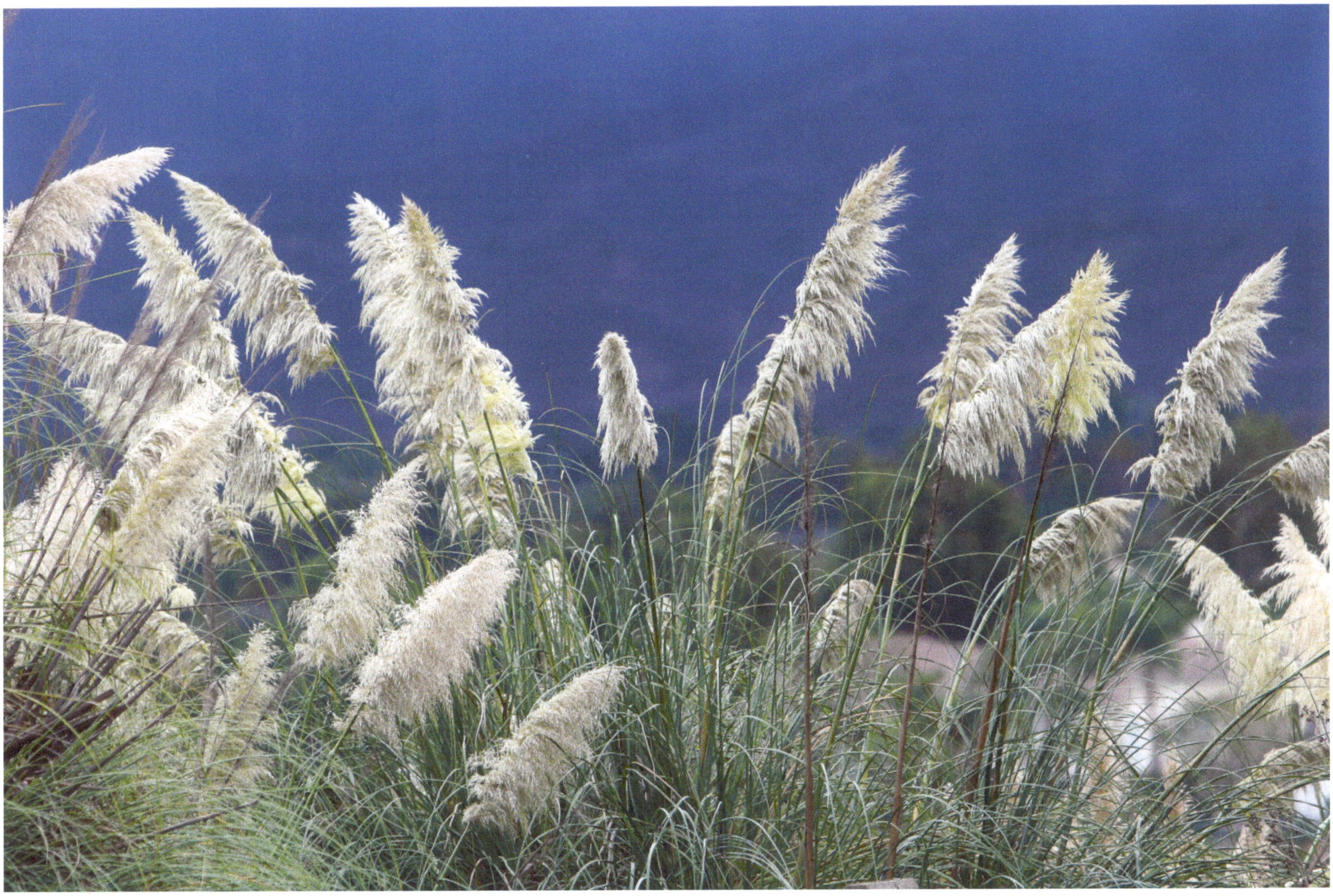

Tall, feathery plumes
sway in the whispering wind,
moving to the rhythm
and the energy
of earth's abundant elements.

They soak in the light of the day,
blessed by nature.

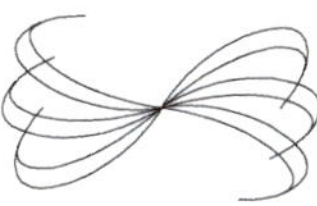

Meditation: Find a place in nature where you can take off your shoes and feel the earth beneath your feet. Visualize the earth's elements flowing upward through the soles of your feet, grounding you and filling your body with the love of Mother Earth.

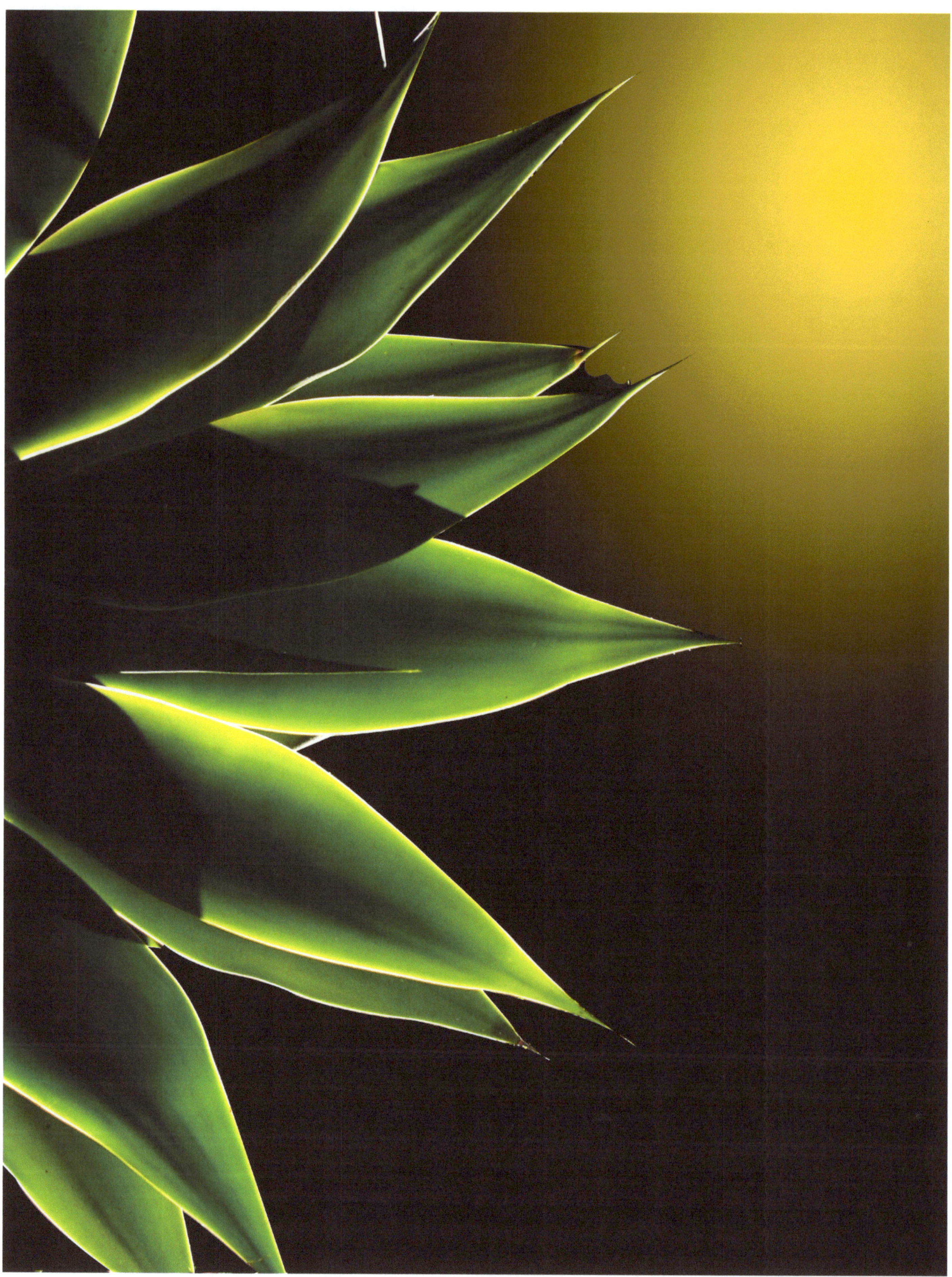

Glowing leaves backlit by the brilliant sun
catch my eye as I walk about.

I feel the warmth of the sun energize me.
I am now glowing just like the leaves.

The light and the leaves join as one,
capturing the image in many different ways,
yet it is this one that captures my heart.

I move on after savoring the sweet moment,
knowing I can delight in this abundance
whenever I desire.

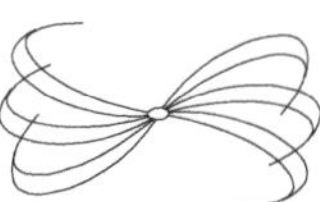

Meditation: Sometimes things catch your eye in a unique way. Look around you. Find something that stands out and focus on it. Why did this object catch your eye? Focus on that unique quality. It will become something you remember, something that makes you feel good. Breathe in and out, allowing each breath to stimulate your creative expression and vision.

Today's promise...

Be present.

I will open my eyes... and see,

I will listen intently... and hear,

I will delight in every delicious morsel... and taste,

I will experience the slightest touch... and feel.

As I take in all the sensual pleasures,

I will surrender

to each sensation...

as if for the very first time.

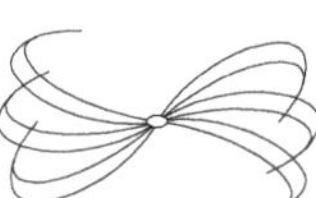

Meditation: Sensory stimulation is all around you. Allow yourself to feel the air as it caresses your skin. Notice if it is cool or warm. Next, listen to the sounds around you, picking one in particular to focus upon. Move on to observe the visual details of your surroundings. Find something to touch; feel it in such a way that you are aware of the texture, the temperature, and any other tactile details. Finally, take a small taste of food or drink. Notice the flavors as they roll over your tongue. Experience the texture, the temperature, the unique taste. The more present you become –even when doing the simplest things each day— the more aware you become in all areas of your life.

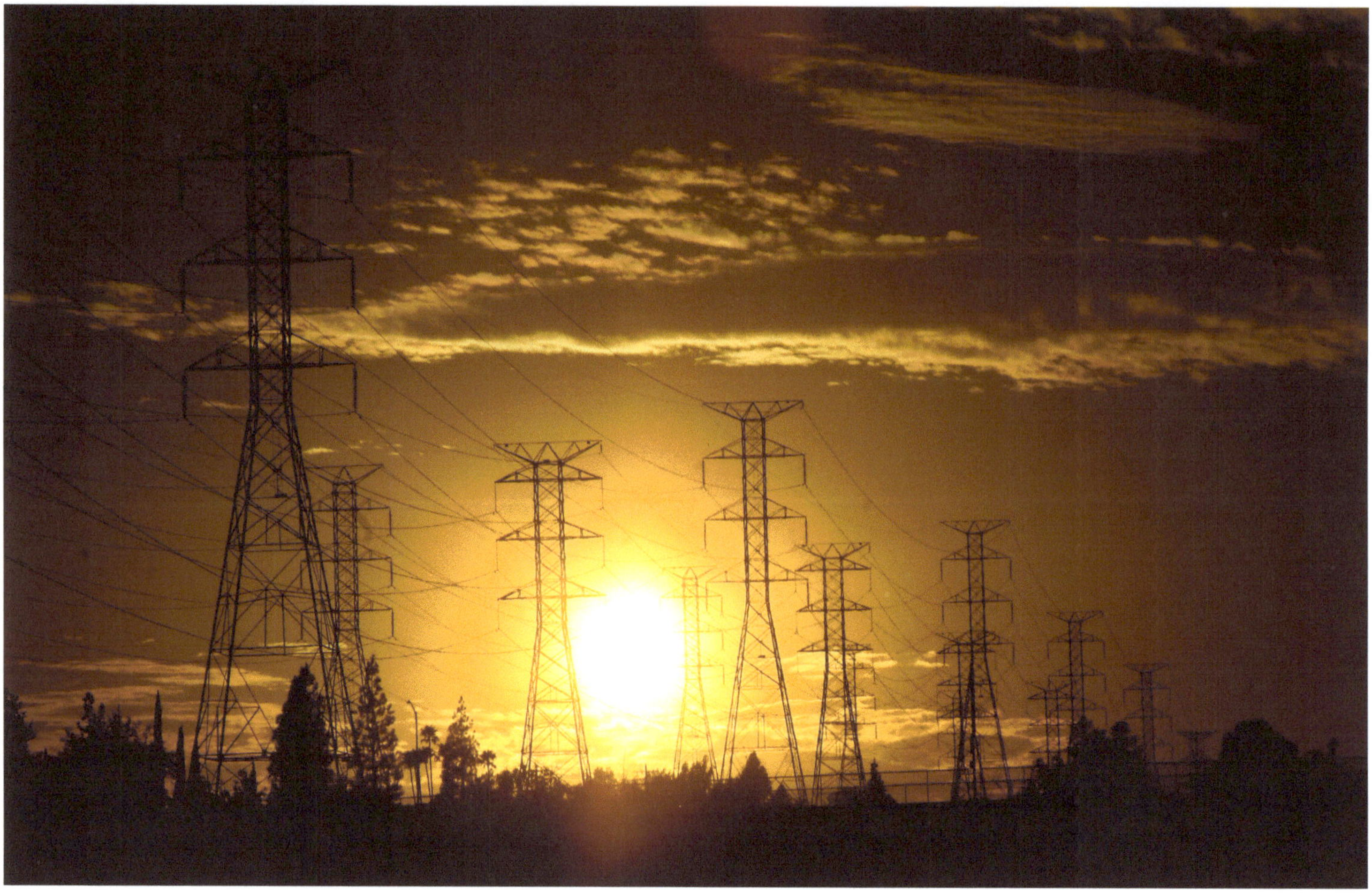

Sunlight streaming, imparts a golden glow
behind backlit silhouettes in a variety of shapes.

Long shadows in the morning give way to
warm light in the late afternoon and evening.

The white glow from a full moon,
or black on black shadows in the night... with just a hint of light.

Patterns,
reflections,
abstract shapes.

There is beauty everywhere.

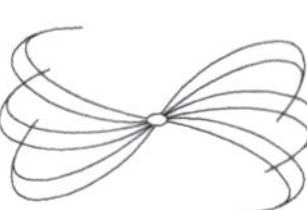

Meditation: Close your eyes and think of all the things you are grateful for in this moment. Acknowledge the abundance and beauty surrounding you. Everything is there to awaken you. Even if just for a moment, take the time to focus on something you appreciate. A great morning practice is to allow yourself to journal freely, letting your thoughts flow for 3-5 minutes while opening your heart to all the gifts in your life.

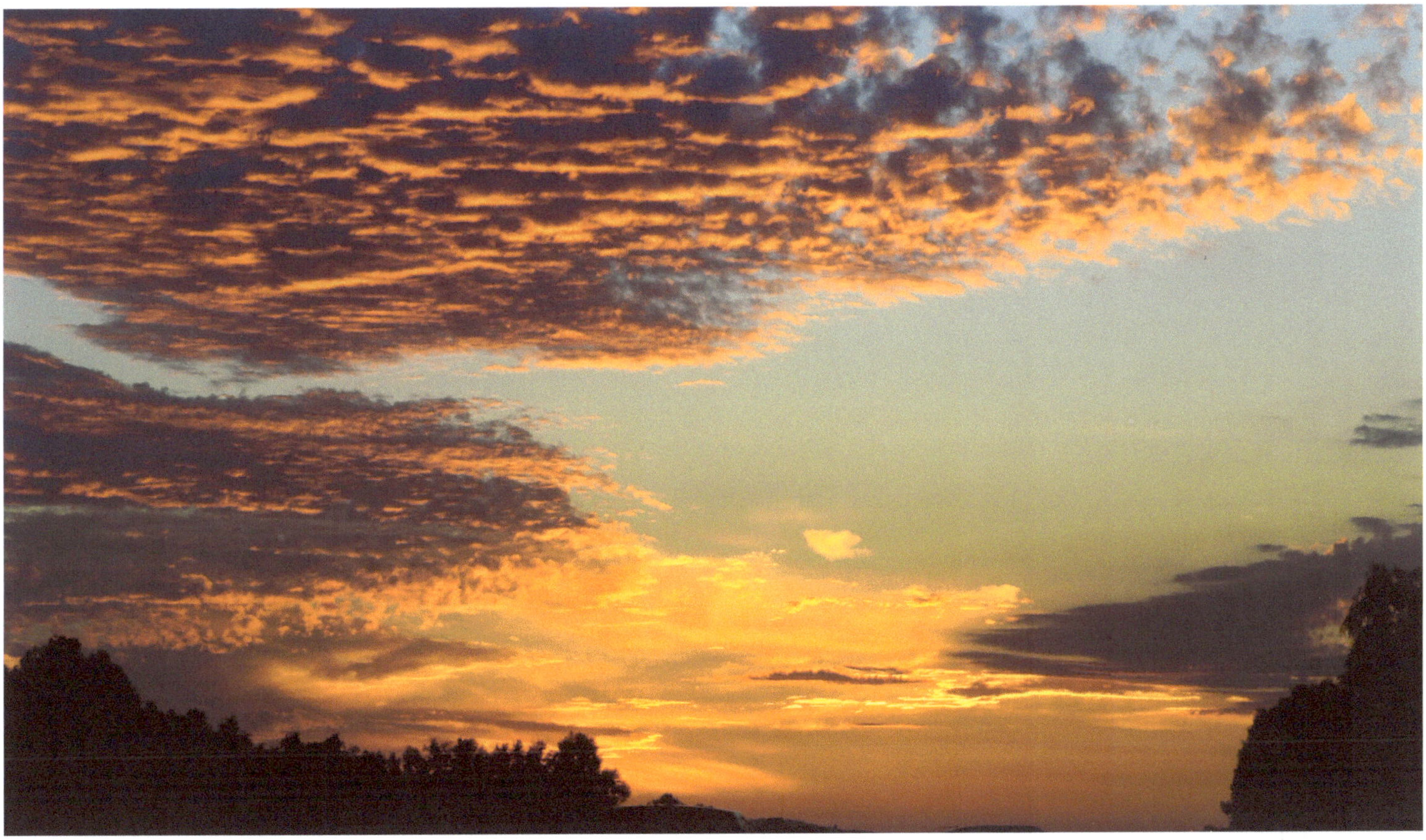

There is nothing more amazing
than the many expressions of the sky.

The calm feeling that accompanies
the enchanted blue of early night,
with billowy white, dimensional clouds
in all shapes and patterns
refracting the light.

These are skyscapes that delight
and bring endless joy.

Gratitude is abundant
through the magic and wonder
of the open skies.

It is nature's artistry,
filling our hearts with awe.

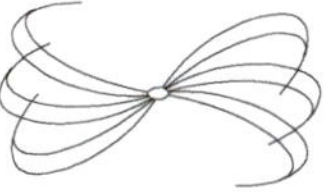

Meditation: Observe the colors all around you, for they offer many moods and feelings. Imagine your favorite colors as you reach deeply into your heart, feeling the emotions associated with them. Allow the color of your choice to flow throughout your body, filling it with energy. Be present, feeling the corresponding emotion—just allow it to be.

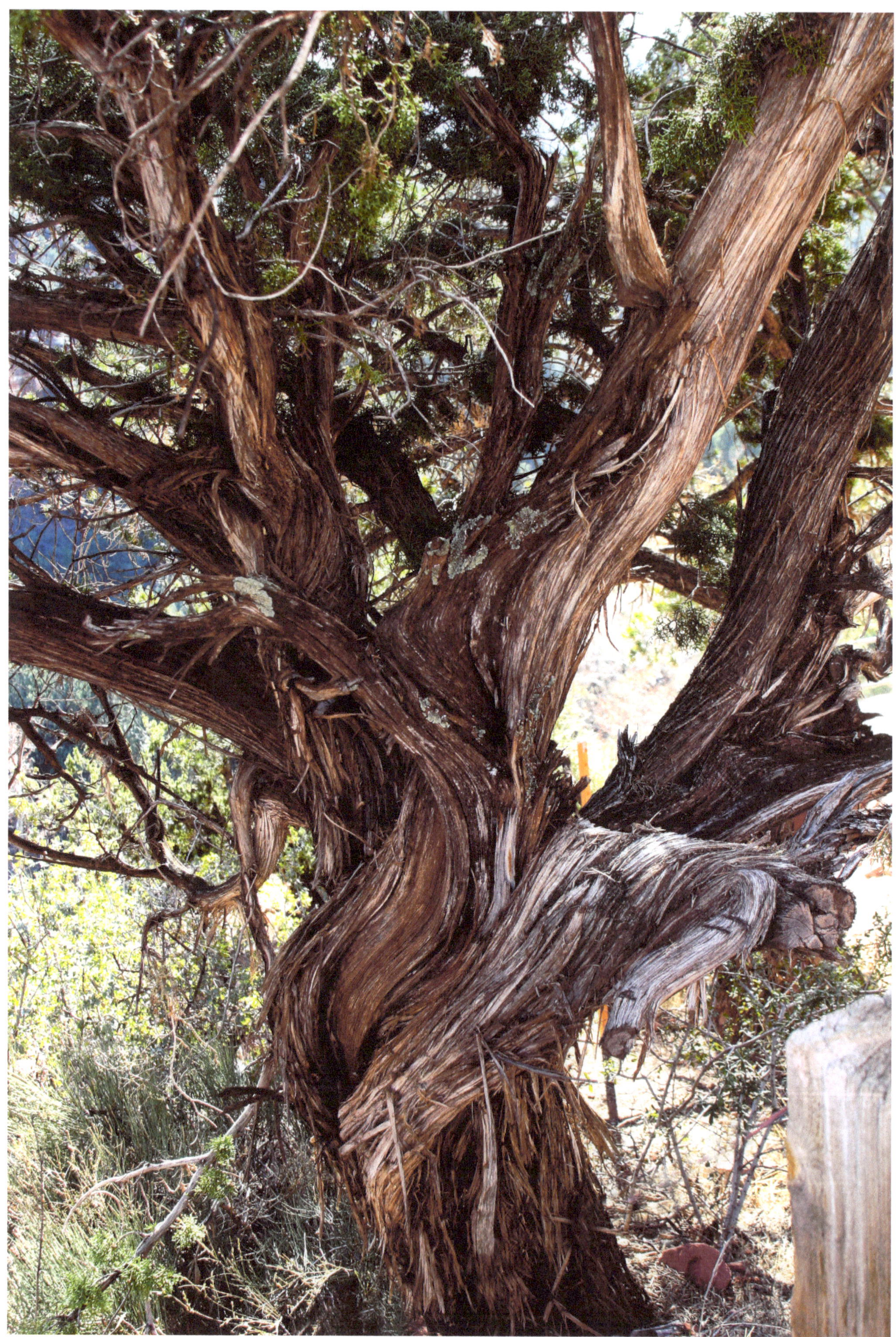

Shapes and patterns are all around us,
wherever we look.

Each has its own unique style,
much like our individual personalities.

Every one of us has a different perspective,
for that is what makes us who we are
and gives us our character.

Be yourself...
trust yourself,
and most of all...
love yourself.

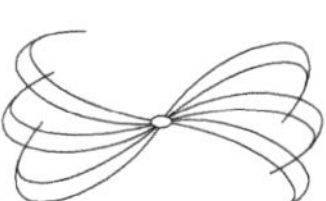

Meditation: Think of things you like about yourself. Focus on the positive, being grateful for all you are. Now, think of your potential with loving kindness. We each have qualities like no other. You are special and one-of-a-kind... a true miracle.

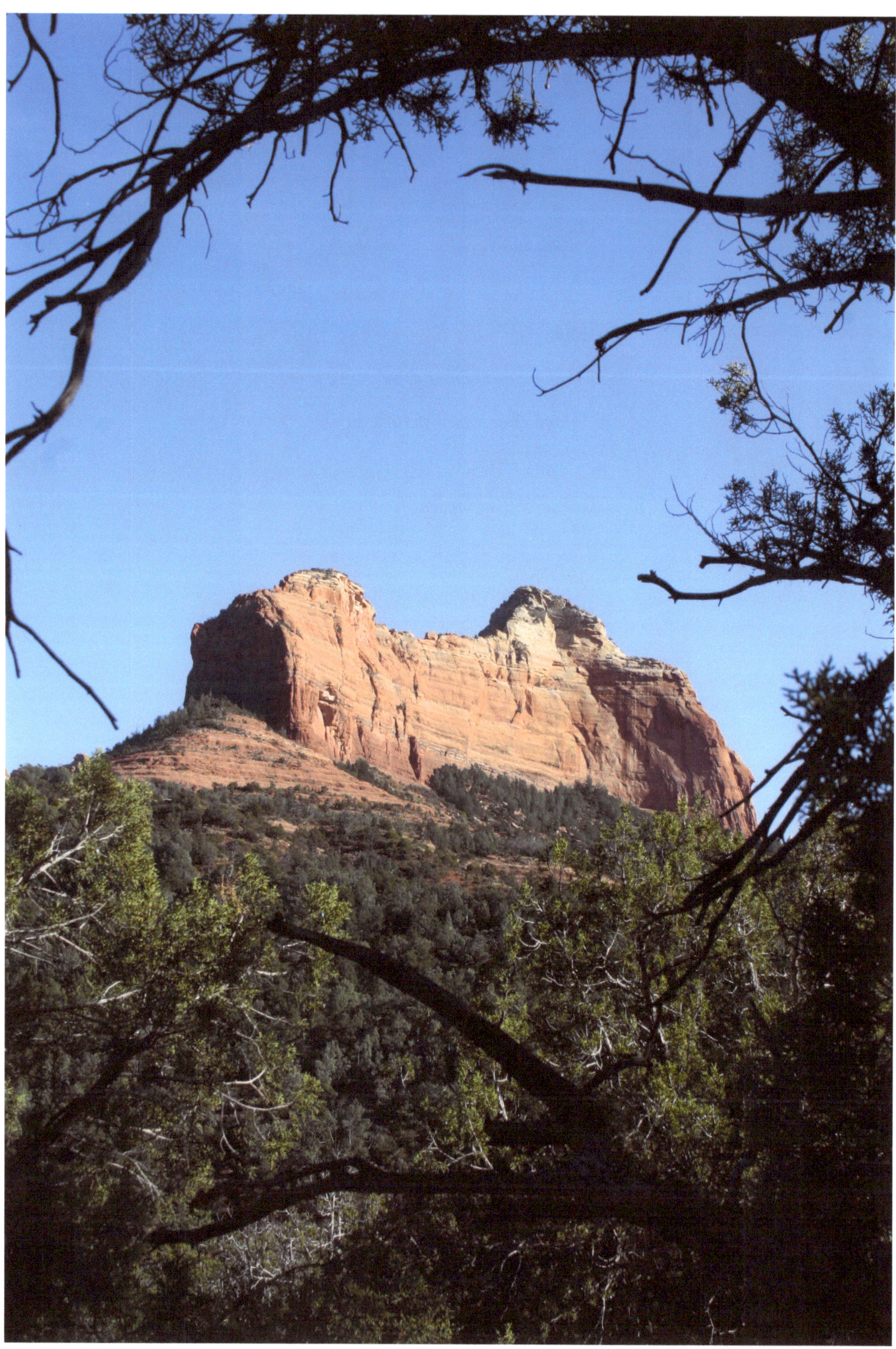

Sometimes, when our vision is obscured,
we have a difficult time accomplishing what we desire.

All it takes to see things more clearly
is a shift in how we view the obstacles.
We just need to frame them in the right way.

When we are in the present moment,
there is greater opportunity
for our direction to become clear.

Only then can we honor the gifts presented to us.

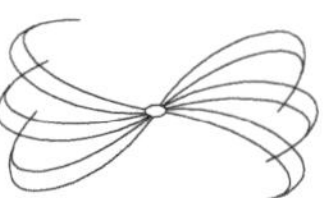

Meditation: Sometimes we're bothered by things that obscure our view. Instead of allowing frustration to take hold, move a little to the left, right, up or down and let the foreground add to your vision. Spend some time thinking about various obstacles in your life. Now consider ways to incorporate these obstacles into your vision. You may find they are actually gifts that become your solution.

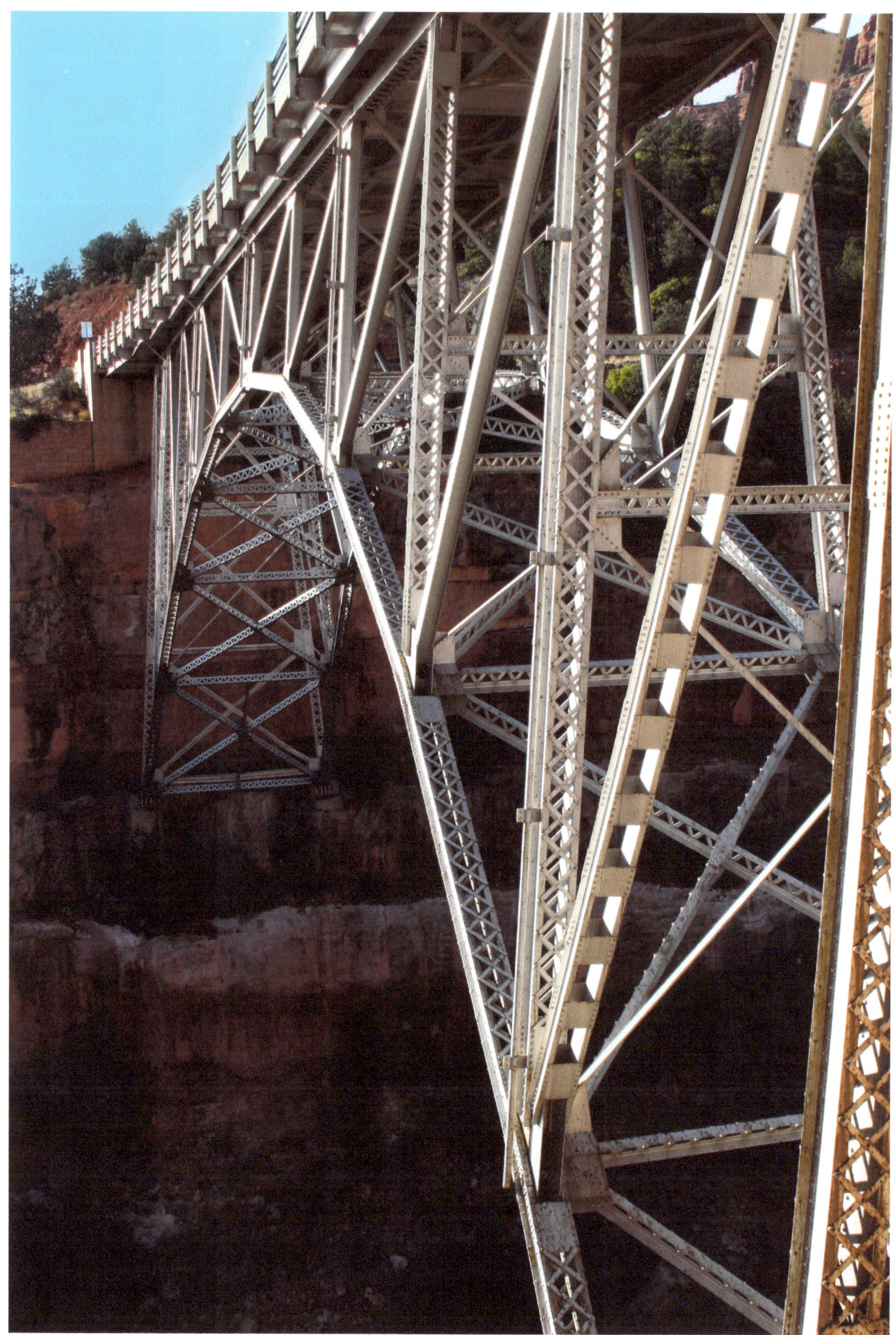

See different,

think different,

and really feel it.

Look closely,

or stand back.

Look above,

or look below.

Sometimes, it is right before your eyes.

Allow creative thoughts and visions to flow.

Be inspired.

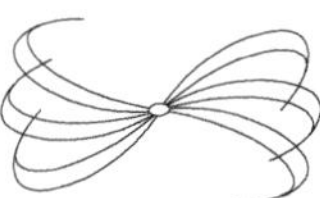

Meditation: Take time to look at things from a different perspective. Look up, look down, sit on the ground, or climb to a high point and look out. Most of us spend too much of our time looking at things as we always have. Give yourself the gift of shifting into new ways of feeling and being.

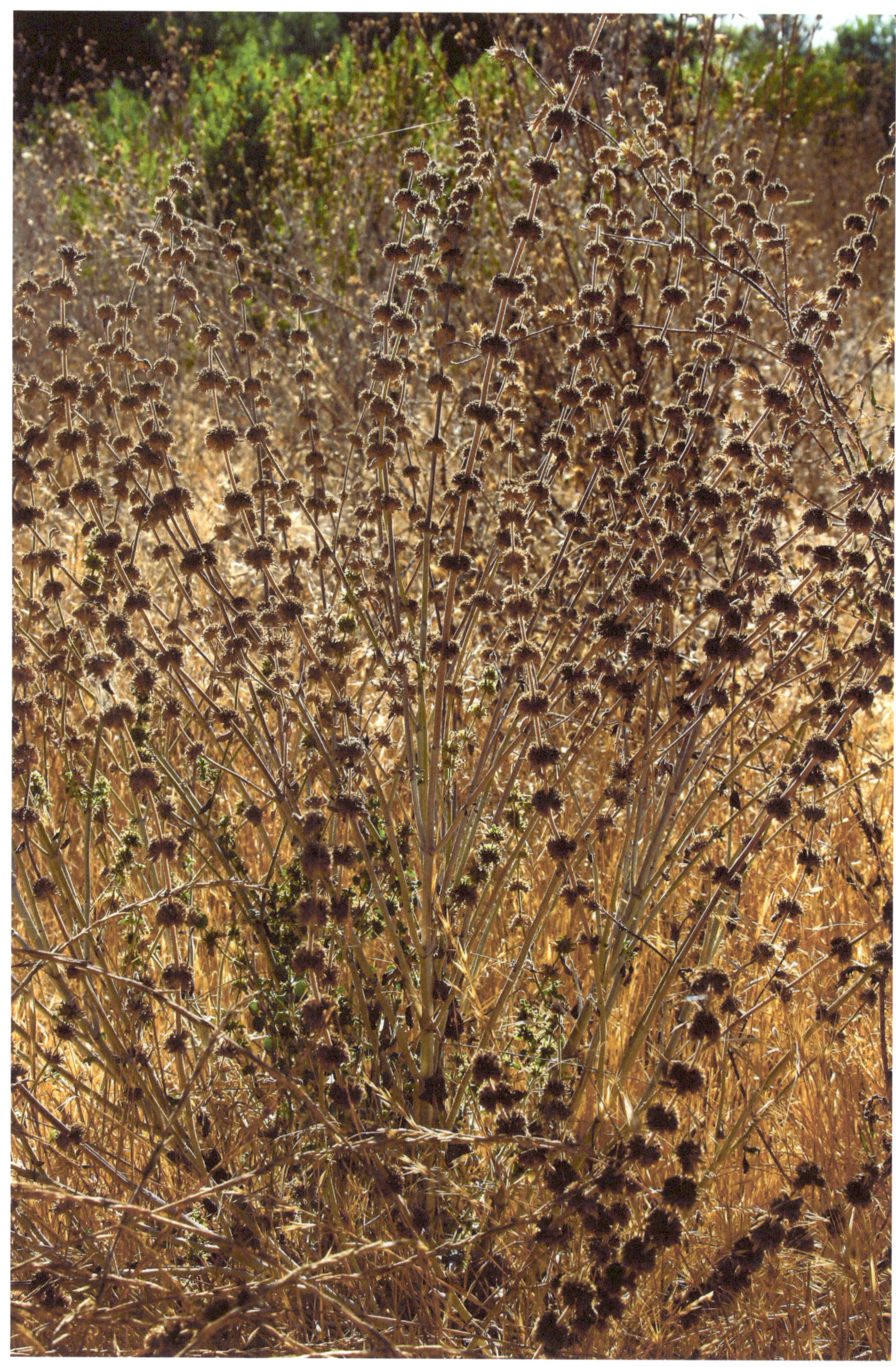

Often our vision seems cluttered,

but sometimes that clutter is just what we need to see.

Pause for a moment,

feeling the chaos.

What does it consist of?

What is necessary?

What is noisy?

What is prominent?

What is in the background?

The problem may not be the clutter,

but rather what we allow it to mean.

Find the beauty...

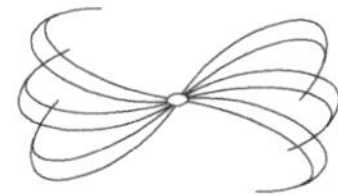

Meditation: Look at the clutter in your life. Clutter can be physical, emotional or psychological. Pick one aspect and filter through it. What are you holding onto? What are you making it mean about you? Is there an underlying theme that links your answers together? Visualize yourself discarding the things that don't serve you and focus on what feels right.

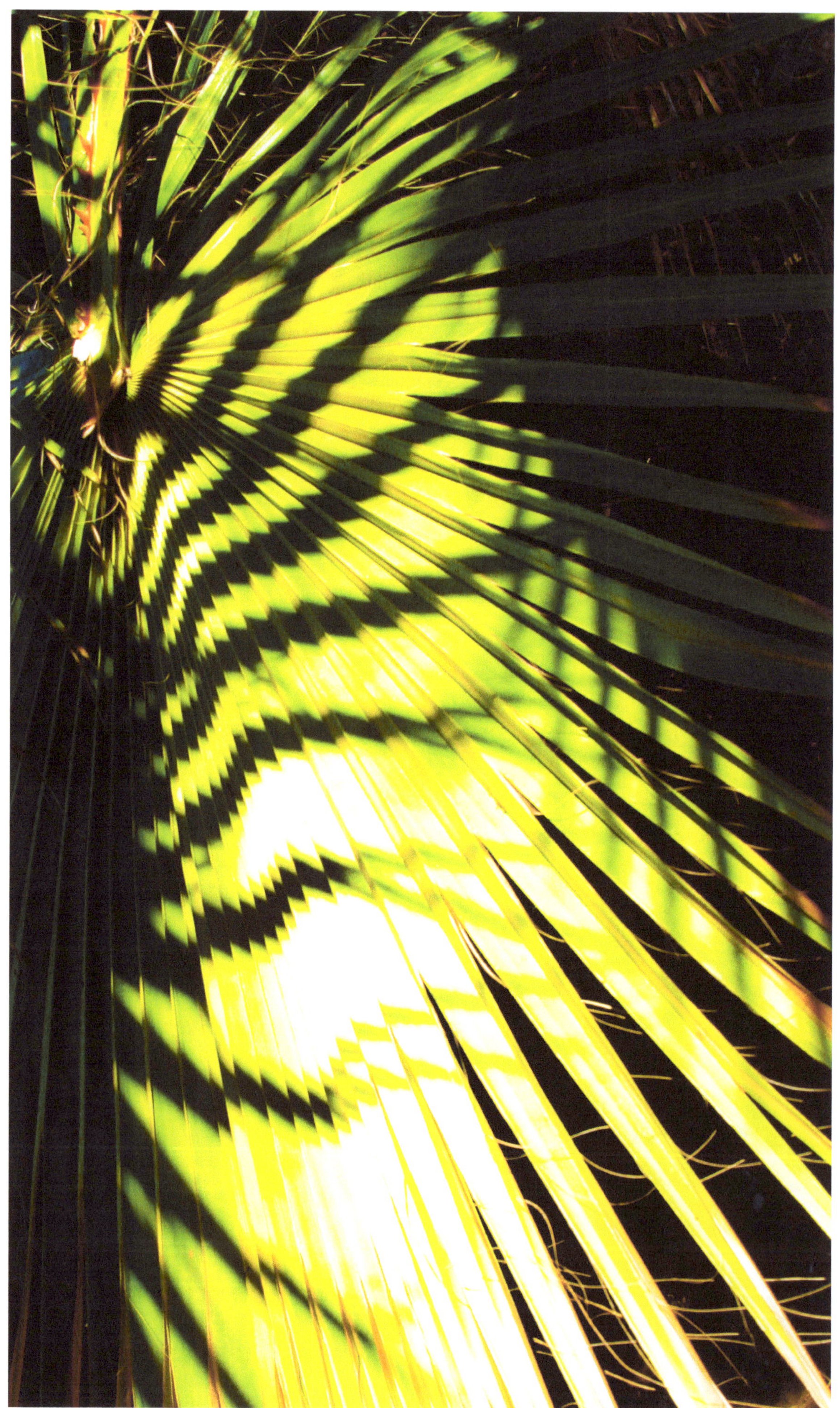

I have always seen much beauty in light,
and now I know why.

Light is positive energy.
It is powerful,
It is peaceful,
It is beautiful,
It is love,
It is the answer.

Whenever I see the light
illuminating anything or anyone,
or casting shadows,
it has a profound effect.

It is the light that will guide me
to where I need to be.

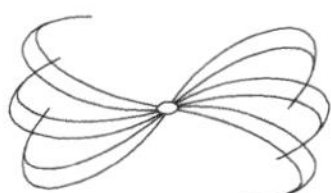

Meditation: Find a place outside where the sun is shining on a textured object. Look at how the light and shadows work together, noting the patterns that form. Remember, there are details in the dark areas as well. Throughout your day, be mindful of shadows around you as well as the interplay of dark and light. Contemplate what you notice in the various objects you encounter.

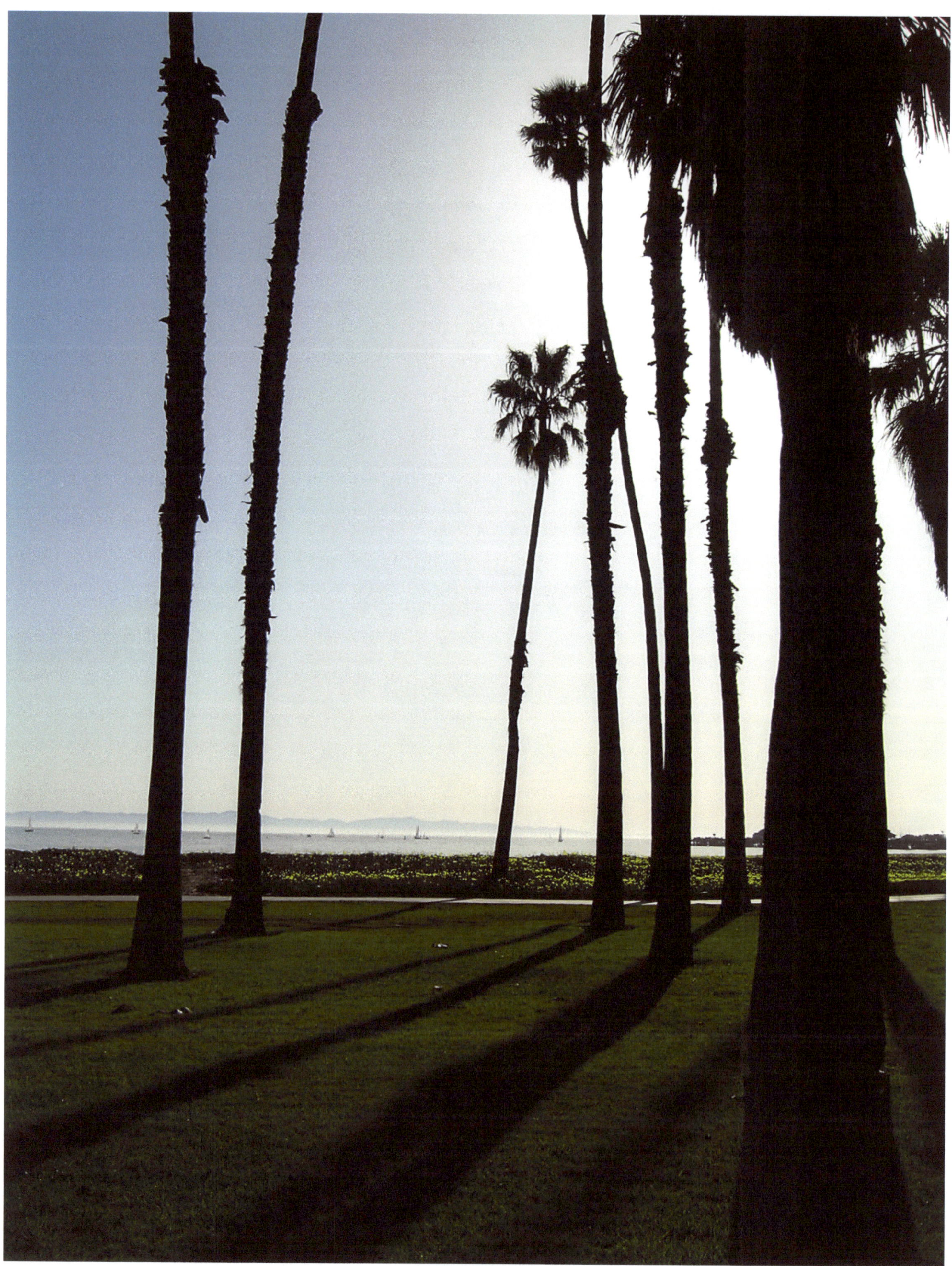

The long shadows of an afternoon sun
stretch across the ground,
creating a wonderful contrast
between the beautiful green grass,
the blue sky and the ocean backdrop.

Each new day gives us another beautiful moment
to enjoy and experience to the fullest.

No matter where
or what our scenery offers,
finding gratitude for the abundance of beauty
provides a feeling of warmth, love and peace.

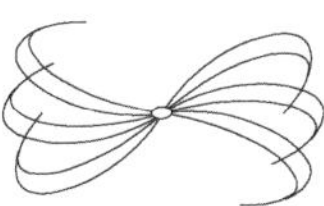

Meditation: Breathe in, "I am tall and mighty like a tree." Breathe out, "I see so much from this view." Open your eyes and heart, see everything. Awareness is part of the journey to discovering you are special. Your unique presence impacts the world.

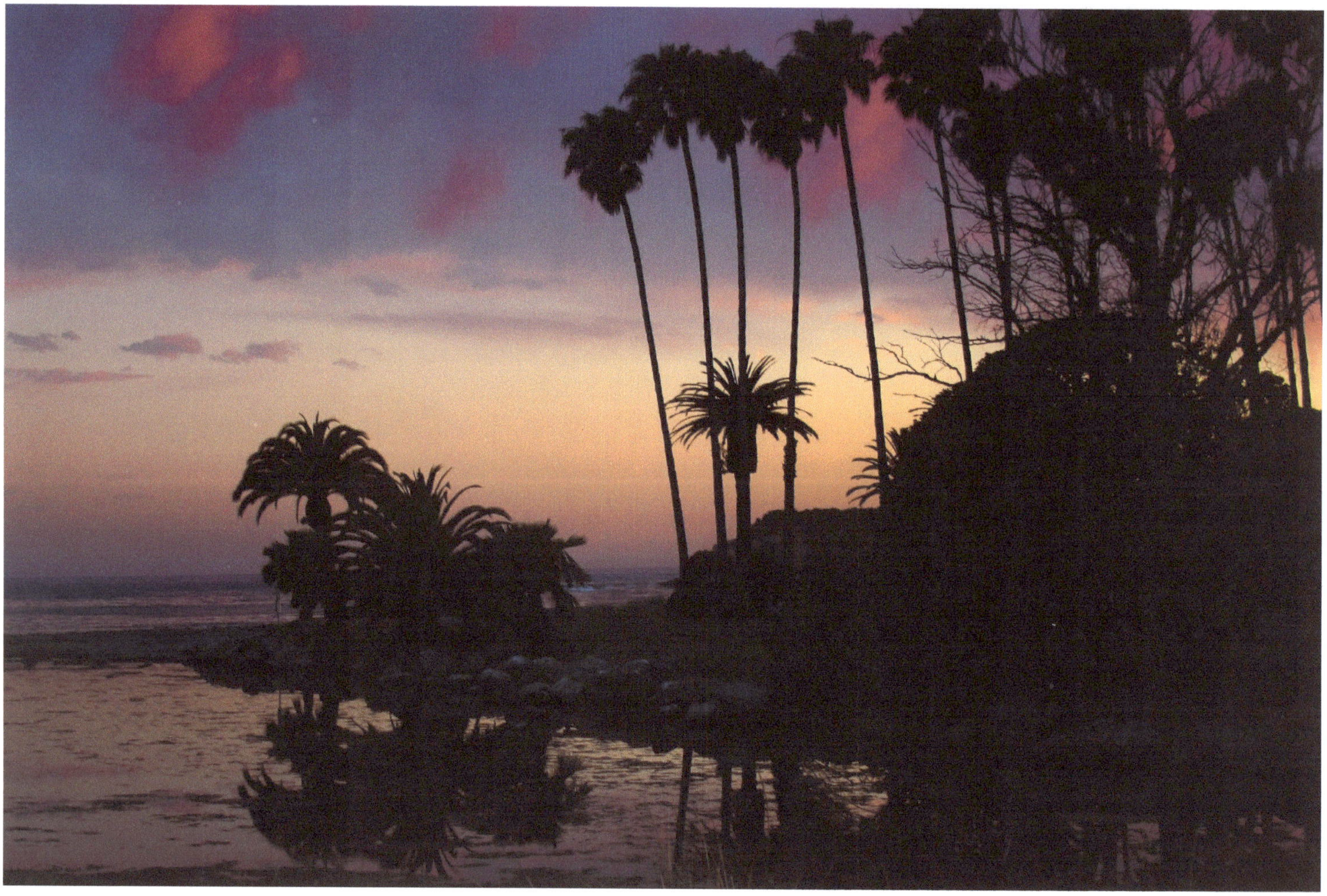

It is early evening
as the muddy water of the lagoon reflects the afternoon sky,
transforming itself into a glorious sunscape.

The silhouette of palm trees and stretch of land
make it truly one of the most beautiful scenes,
taking my breath away.

I feel relaxed in this beautiful setting,
and I feel peace knowing
it is filled with many wonderful memories.

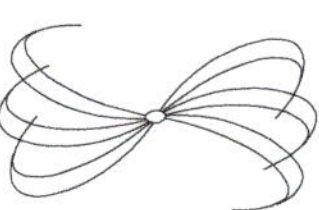

Meditation: There is always an opportunity to find appreciation. Much like this polluted lagoon, if you look long and deep enough, beauty will be revealed. Unpleasant people and situations confront us every day. Step back for a moment, tuning in to one positive aspect about the person or situation. You will be delighted to experience appreciation and gratitude rippling to all areas. It always comes back to you in surprising ways.

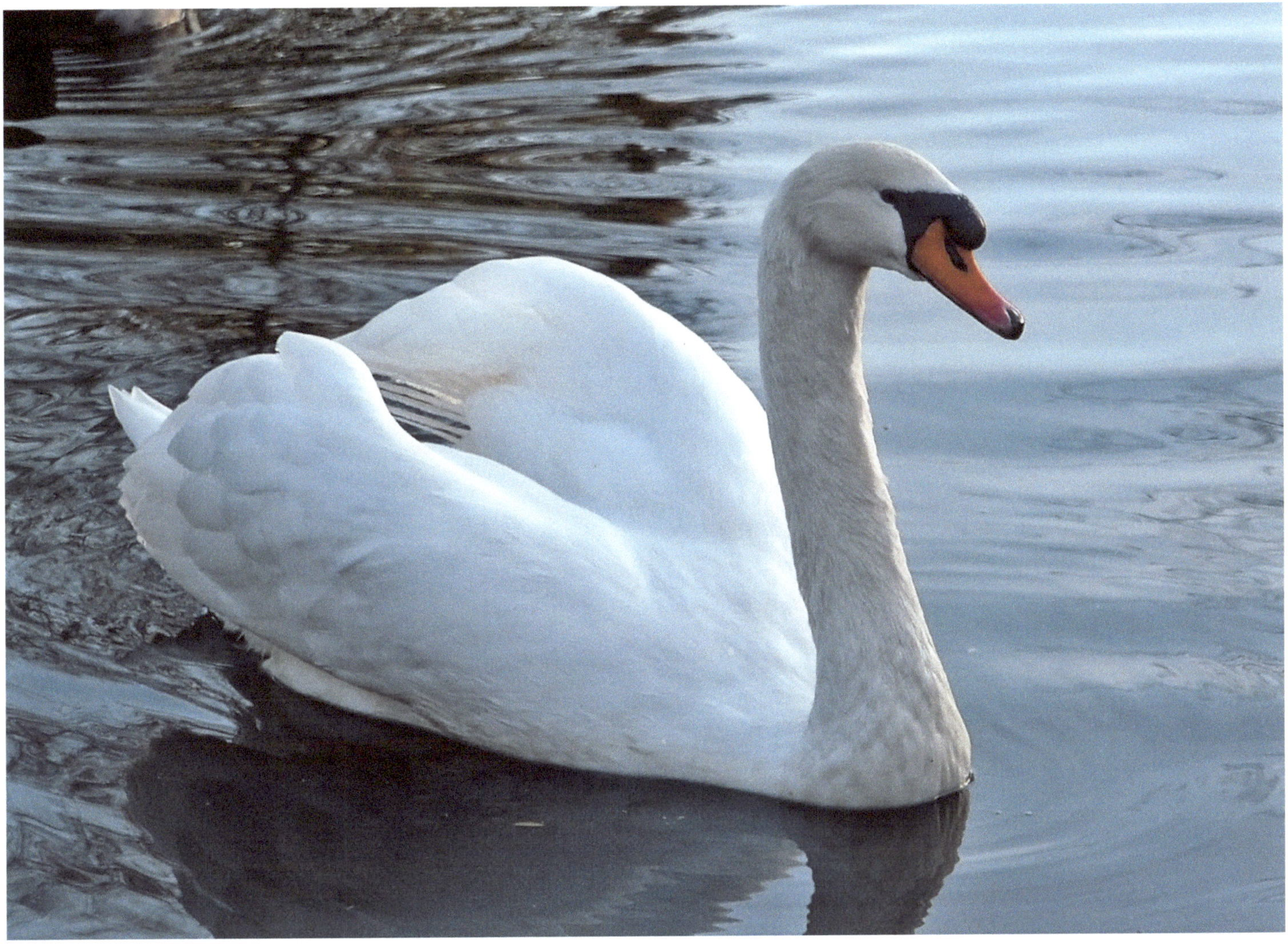

Living peacefully,

I am beautiful,

I am loved.

I am.

Flowing gracefully,

with an open mind,

experiencing each and every moment.

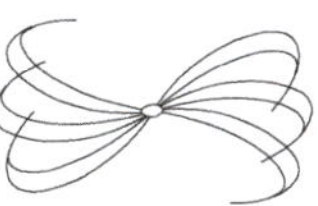

Meditation: Find a quiet place to sit where you will not be disturbed. Imagine a time when you were truly relaxed and at peace. Close your eyes and recall the details of the experience, allowing yourself to feel the peace of the memory. Embrace the peace in this moment, holding it as long as you desire. Sustain this feeling even after opening your eyes. Carry this peace with you throughout your day.

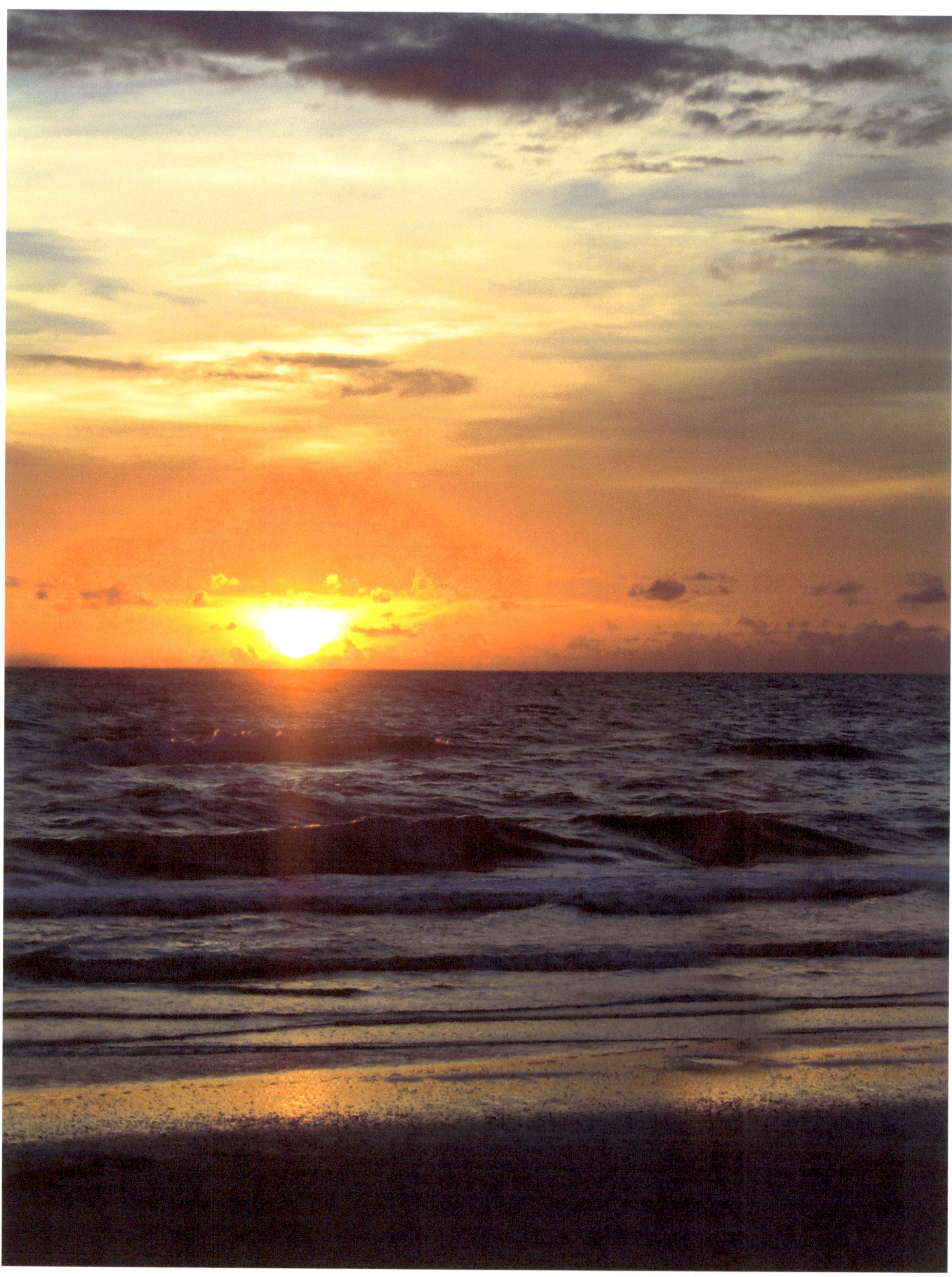

My soul expands
through the wonder of a sunset.

Beautiful,
spiritual,
my heart captures every one
through my camera lens,
never tiring of them.

The rich variety of colors,
the glorious skies that meet the horizon
creating patterns, shapes,
and the glow on the water.

They bring calmness and peace within.

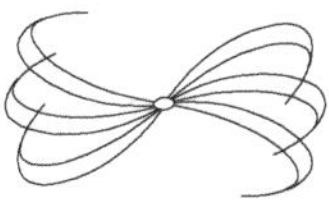

Meditation: Make the time to honor yourself with the gift of a stunning sunrise or sunset. Enjoy all of its glory as it unfolds before you. Notice the feelings that arise, reveling in these emotions.

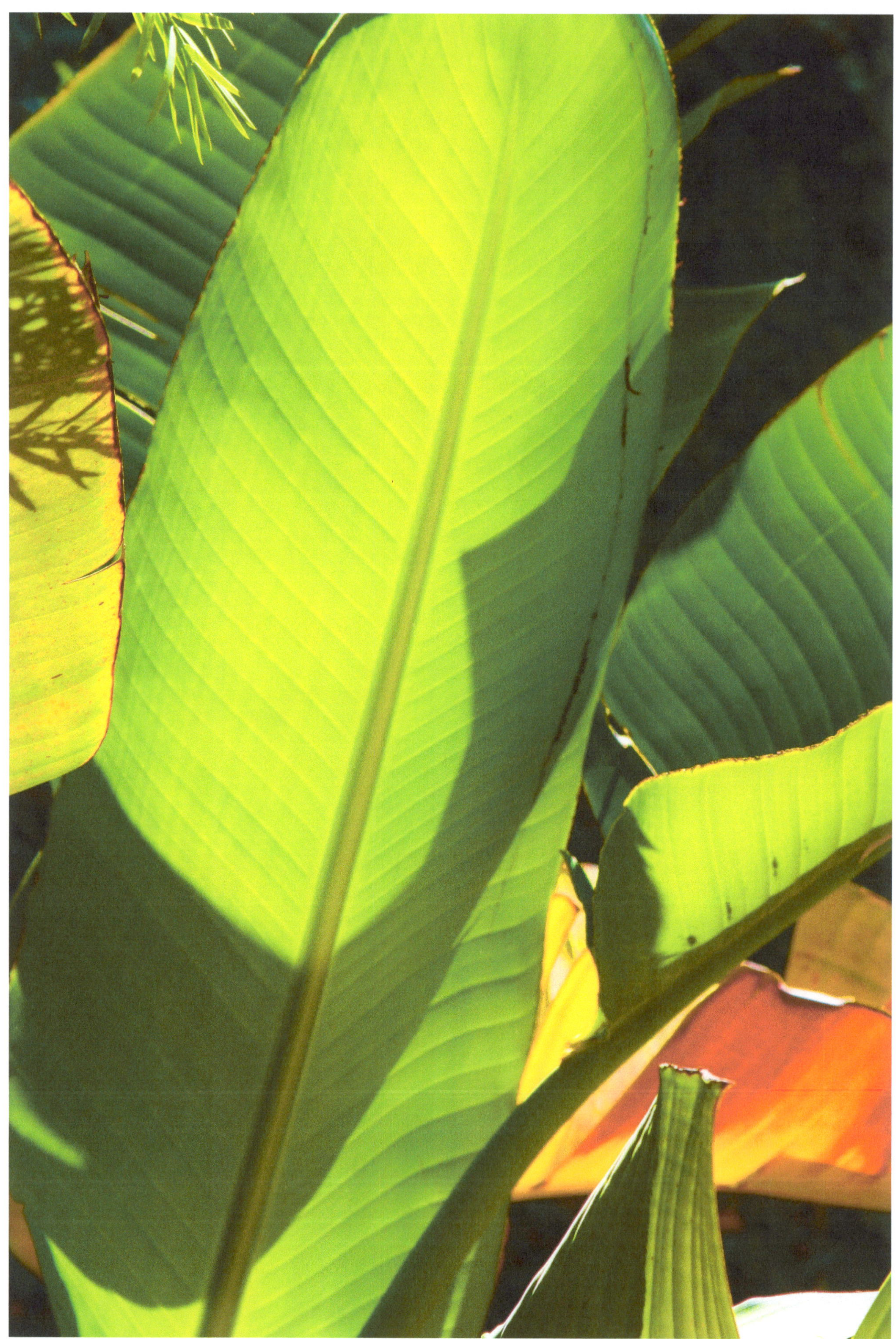

Often things go unnoticed in our everyday life.

Taking time to be in the moment
allows us to be grateful for extraordinary beauty.

And there it was in my garden,
luscious and full of life.
Is it just the way the sun caught it at this moment,
or have I been oblivious
to the colors, the textures and the way it illuminates?

The abstract pattern, the color and hues
make such a captivating treat for the eyes.

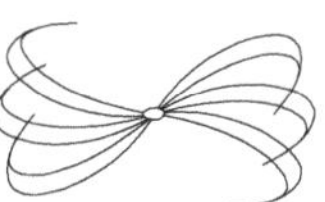

Meditation: In this moment, think of one thing you may take for granted. Is there something or someone you accept as part of your daily routine without acknowledging their specialness? Make it a practice—today and every day—to be mindful of those things around you, and give them your present moment's attention.

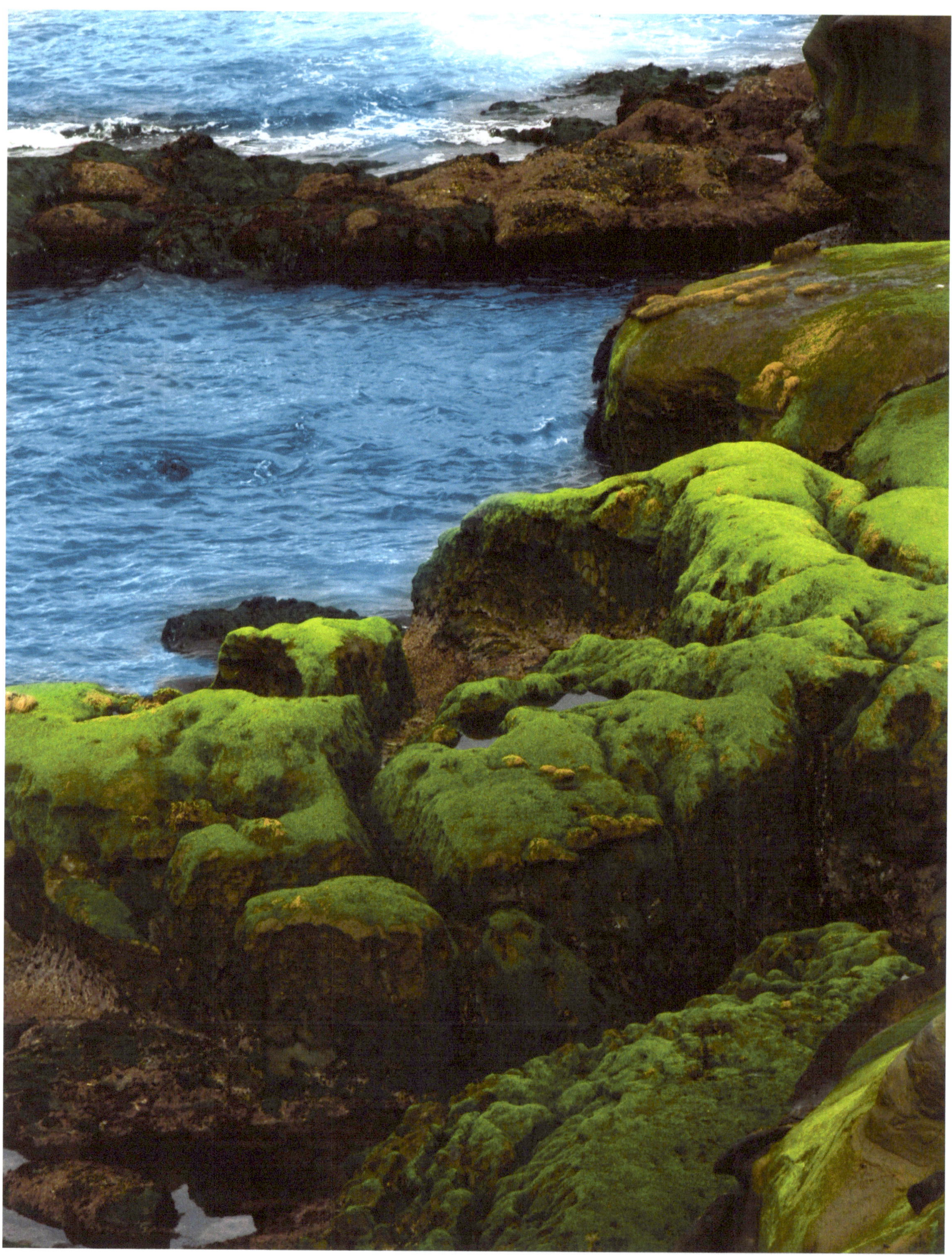

A magical place,

one that offers inner peace and solitude.

As the seasons change, so does its appearance.

The autumn moss is so vibrant and alive

as water splashes against the rocks.

Shapes.

Textures.

Colors.

The energy is strong,

positive

and inspiring.

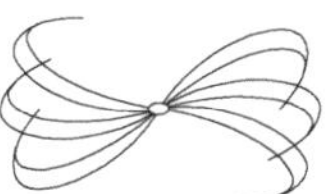

Meditation: Imagine a place that offers you a feeling of serenity. Close your eyes and visualize yourself there. Breathe, letting go and relaxing if only for a few moments. Remember, this feeling can be yours any time. Just go within and connect to it.

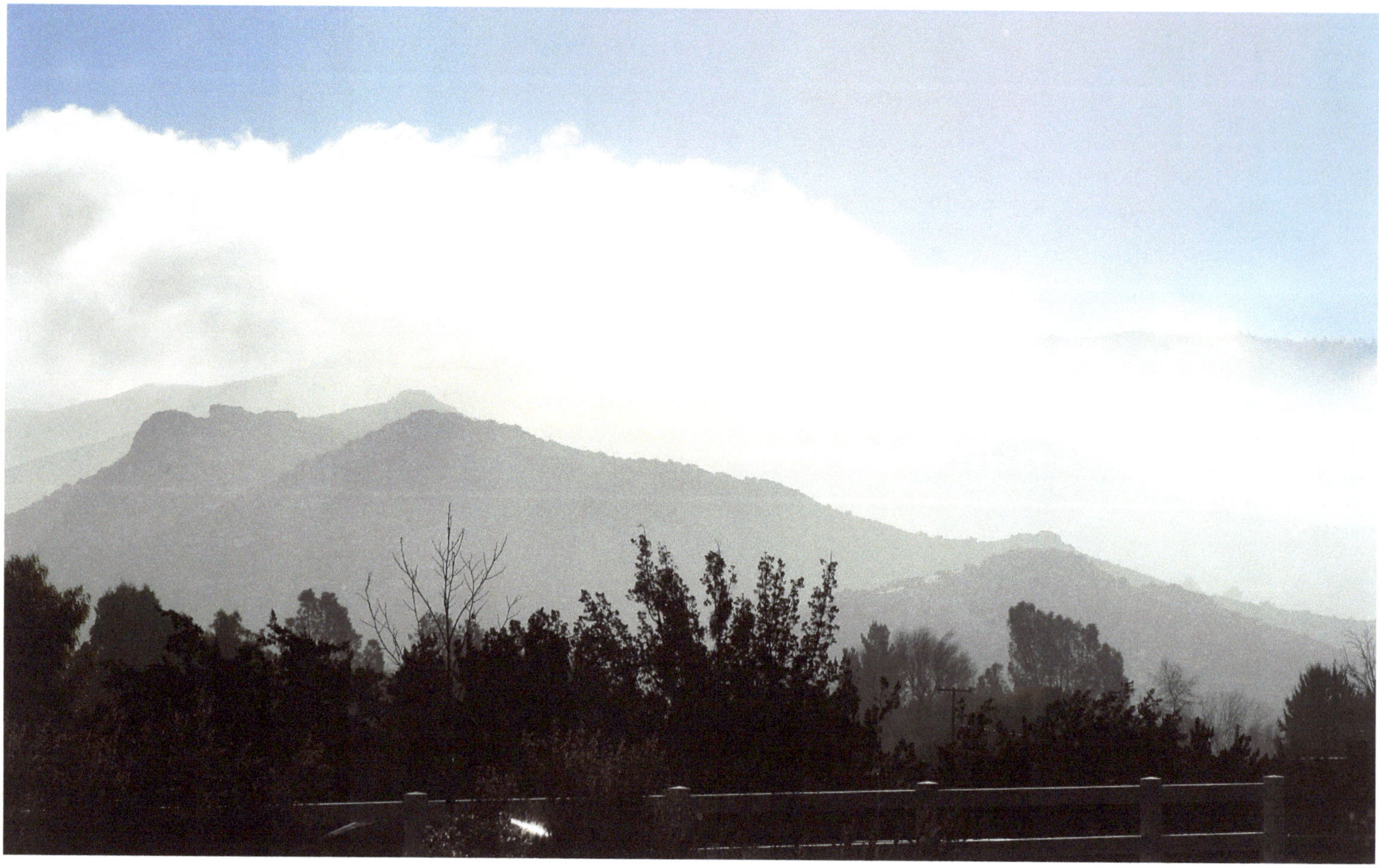

Majestic mountains in the distance,
with soft layers creating infinite depth.

It comes through the fog, haze and light clouds
like a painted landscape,
a wondrous mirage brought to life.

It is my passion to capture this expansive beauty,
becoming one with divine magnificence
in all of its abundance.

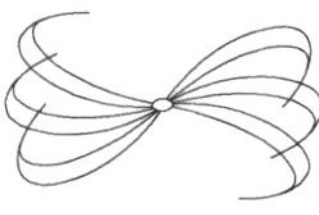

Meditation: The little things you do and experience are just a small part of the bigger picture—your life. We often spend much of our time focusing on the destination, when the most joyous experience is in the journey. Savor the small moments, as they are the ones that count. They joyfully complete your life.

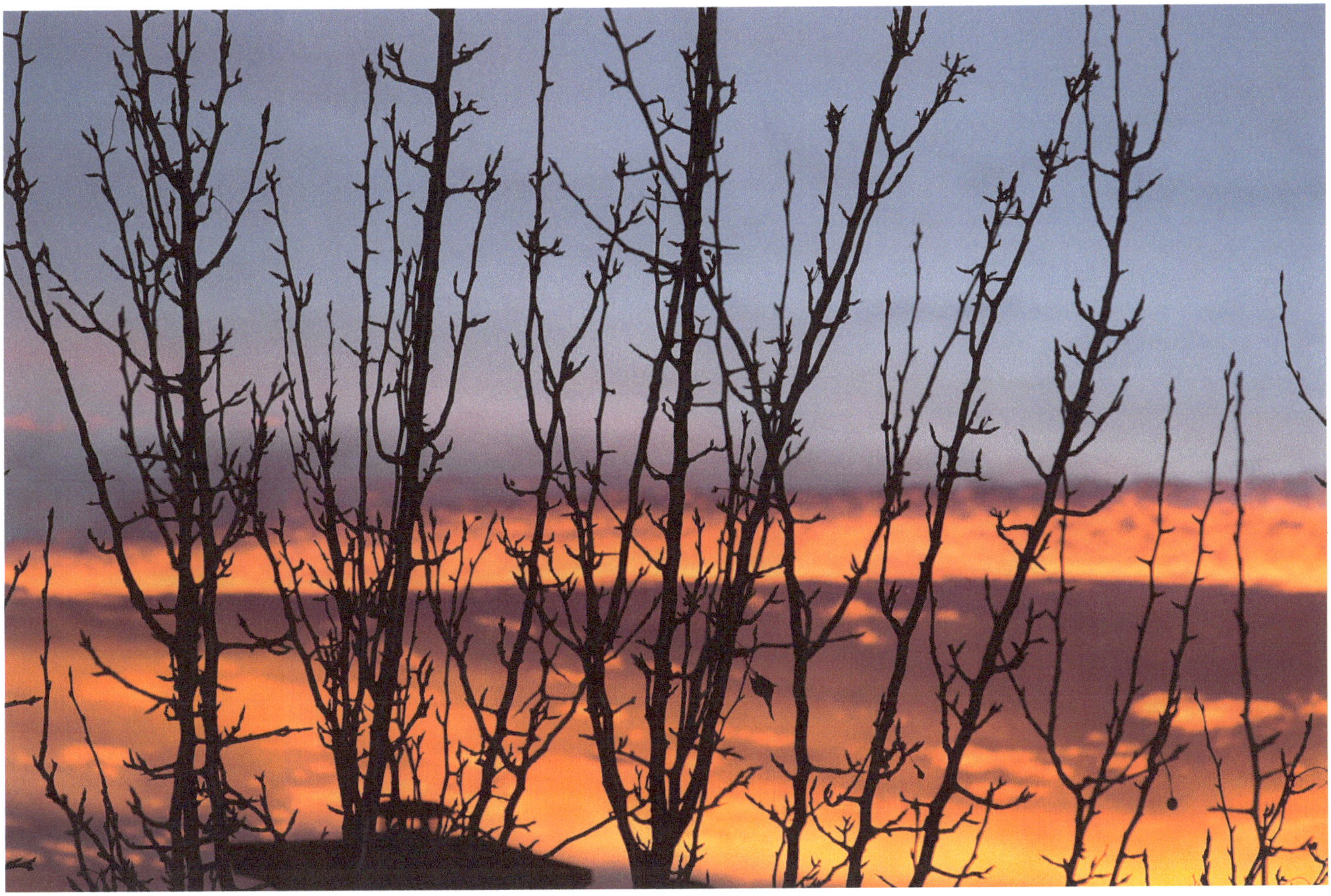

Every morning we are greeted with a new dawn,
inviting us to experience a glorious new day.
The sky was calling out to me
as a reminder to have fun and play.

I knew I only had moments to celebrate this stunning sunscape,
as the exquisite sky would soon disappear.

Thank you, sky, for helping me feel so alive.
I am filled with positive energy and creative vision
to begin my day.

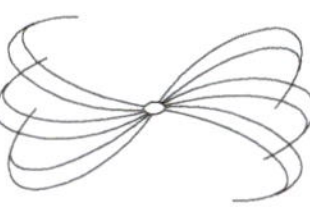

Meditation: Begin each day with gratitude. When you first awaken, go into your heart and allow yourself to connect with something or someone you appreciate. Stay with the feelings for a few moments, experiencing emotions with love and thankfulness. When you feel the exercise is complete, journal about the experience.

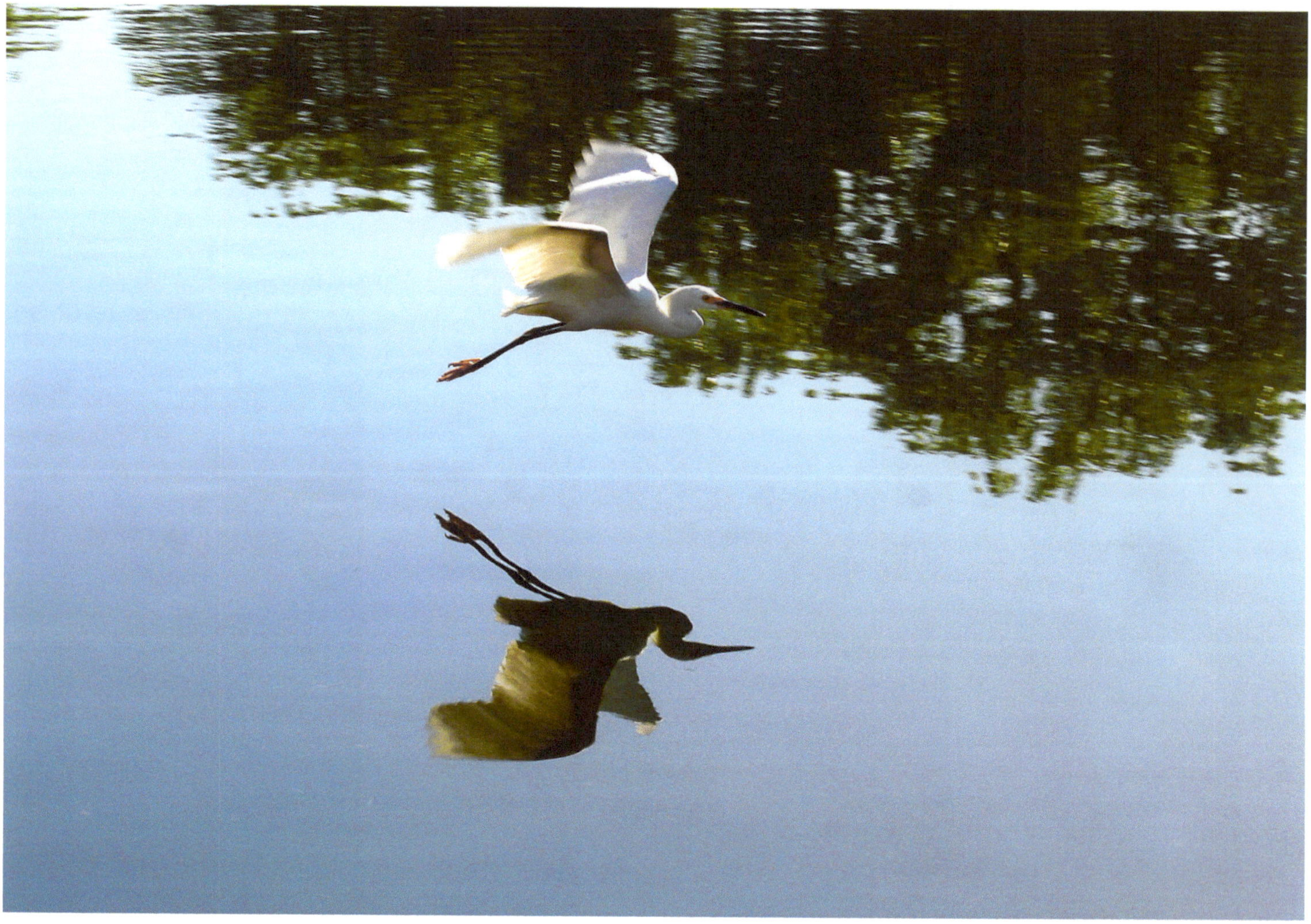

Imagine yourself soaring above it all,

free as a bird,

graceful

and elegant,

gliding above the water,

creating the perfect reflection of tranquility.

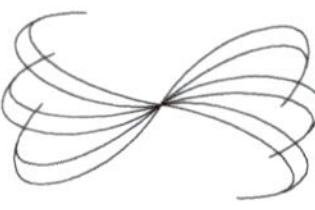

Meditation: We have the free will necessary to try something new and daring, yet we don't often believe in ourselves enough to go for it. Imagine you are there right now, living your dream. Allow yourself to feel it. What is the cost of not living your vision? Peace, love, joy? Create your road map to start living your true potential.

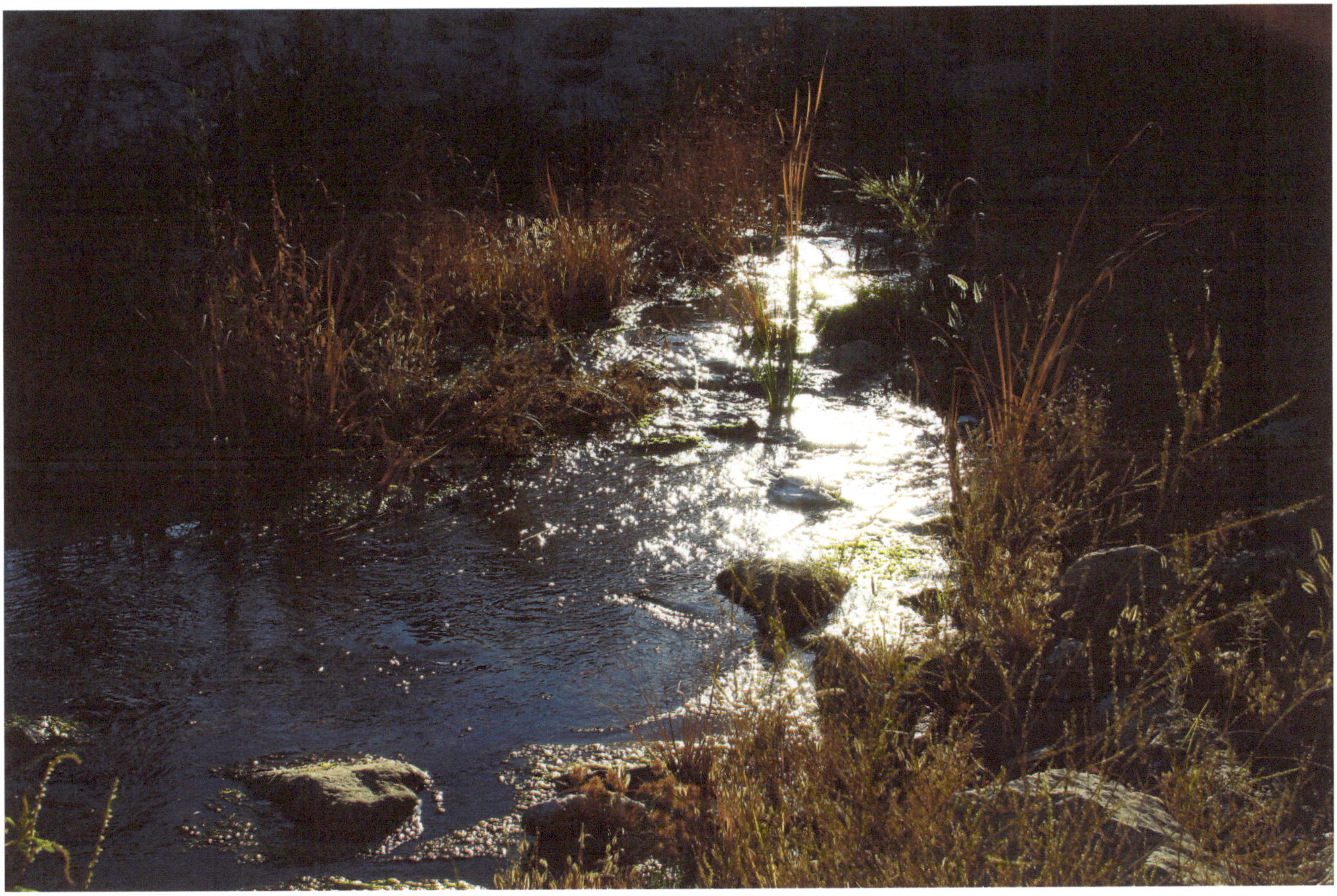

Sunlight glistening on the water,
illuminating the plants growing in the wild.
Glowing, shimmering and full of earthy tones.
It is a symbol of protection and love...
setting the mood for a perfect day.

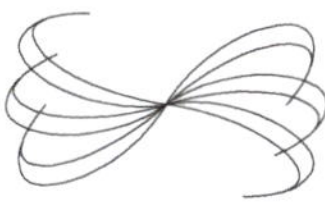

Meditation: Take a walk in silence, paying attention to each step. Notice the sensation of the ground against the bottom of your feet as you roll through one step and on to the next. It doesn't matter where you are going, just experience walking. The awareness of each step is the goal, there is no destination.

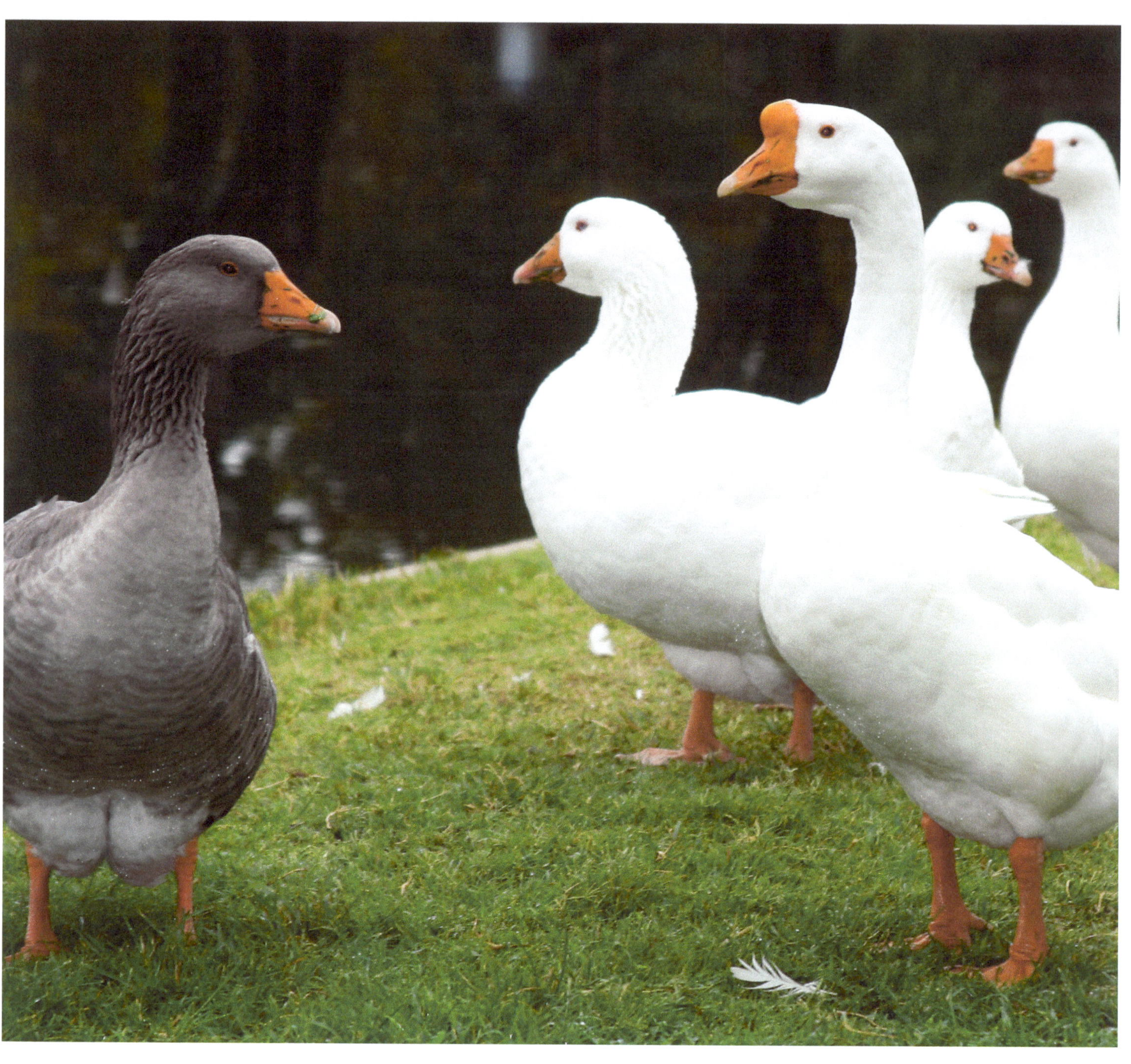

Be yourself, be different, be authentic.
Stand out from the crowd.
When you truly love yourself,
it doesn't matter what others think.

Follow your heart.
Others will stare out of admiration for your courage,
your willingness to be real.

Embrace your individuality.
Diversity is the beauty in the world.

Accept yourself.
Love yourself.
There is no one else quite like you.

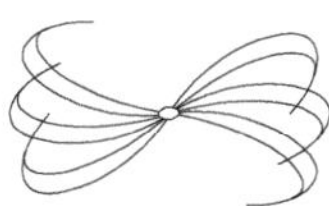

Meditation: We often worry what others think. What would happen if you did what you wanted? You would be in your true essence. Be yourself, love yourself and appreciate all your qualities. Take a few moments and BE with yourself. Look in the mirror and tell yourself you are special and you are loved. Say it through your heart with purpose and conviction.

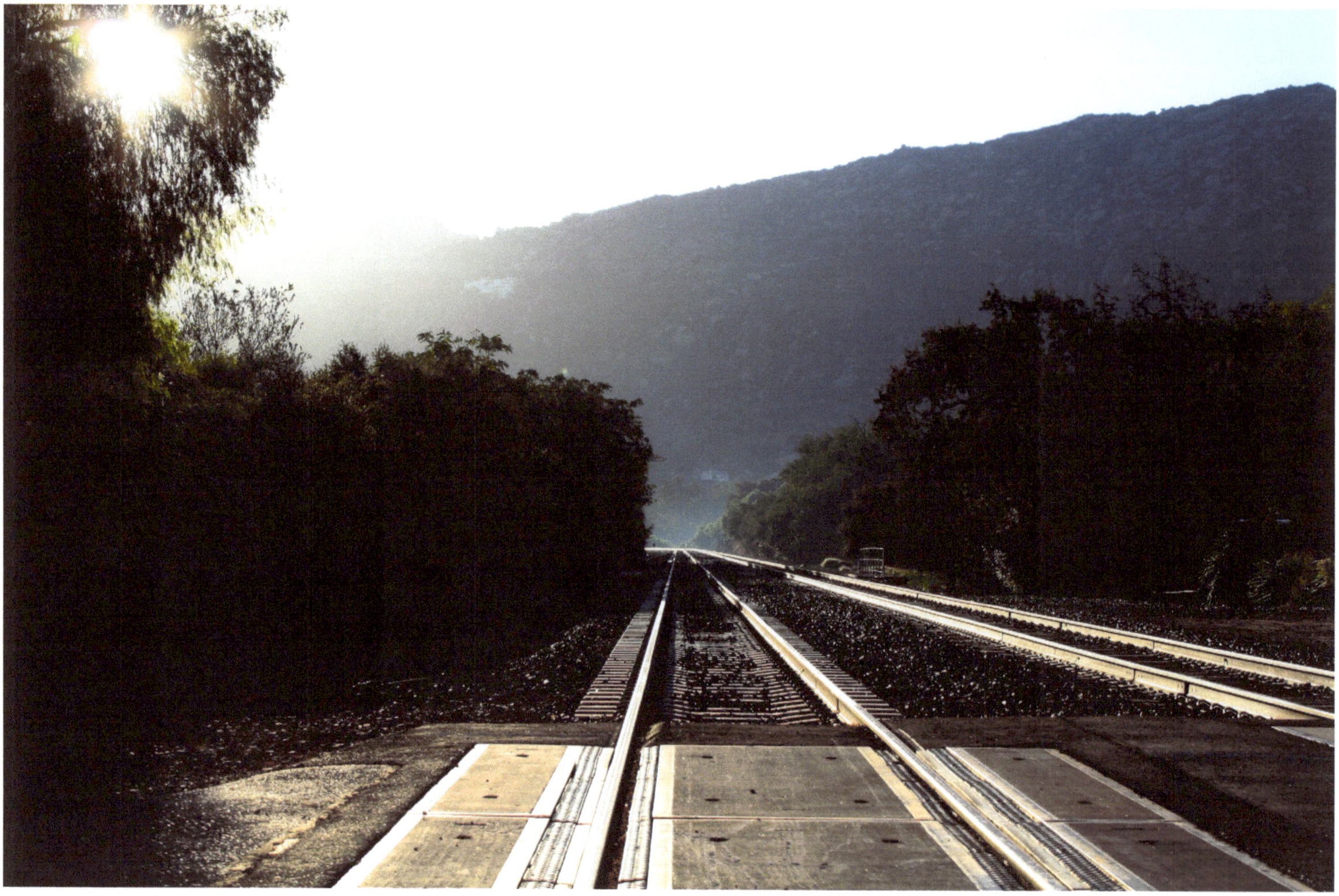

Often times we wait for things to happen,
allowing ourselves to get off track.
Awareness is noticing the difference
between being and doing,
slowing down,
enjoying,
just BEing,
while learning to appreciate each moment.
The greatest gifts are found in the present.
Be here now.

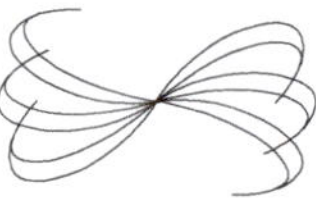

Meditation: What are you waiting for? Allow yourself to release expectations. You can learn lessons from your past and allow the future to unfold naturally, all while living in the present. Practice observing how much time you spend in the past and the future. Be mindful this moment is the one that counts. It is the only one that matters.

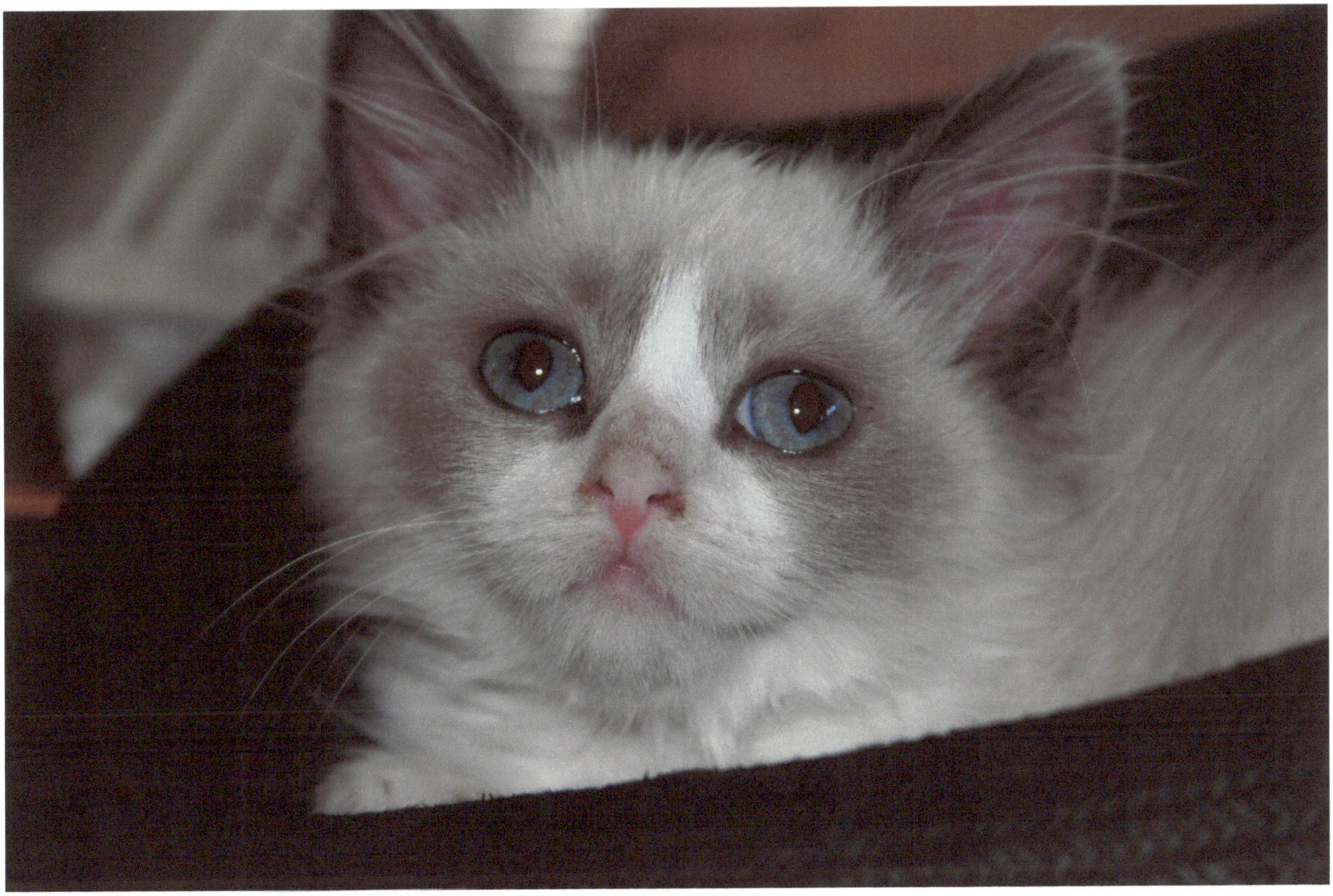

The essence of animals brings us comfort.
When we truly connect to their sweet spirit,
we can learn much from them.

Unconditional love,
playfulness,
and being in the moment.

Looking into the eyes of this kitten,
we feel the emotions of her life,
so beautiful
yet fragile.

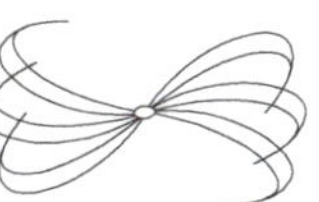

Meditation: Every creature has its own story. We sometimes forget this because we are absorbed in our own world. Whenever an interaction with someone brings out judgment, we have an opportunity to connect with compassion. Ask yourself, "What is their story?" Notice if you feel a shift in your heart. Everyone has a story, just ike you.

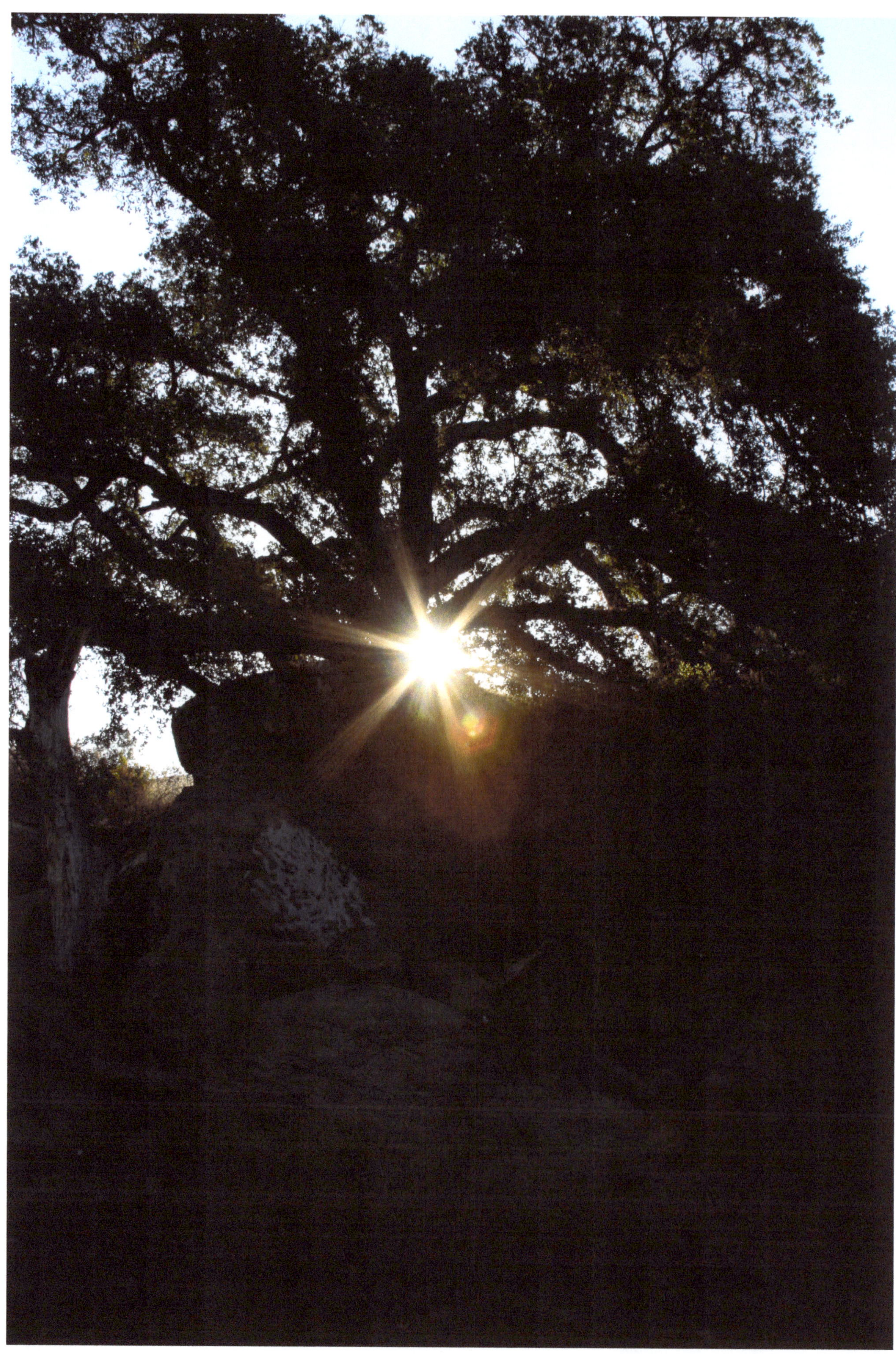

Cool, crisp air,
and grass moist from the morning dew.
I am feeling connected with the energy of the earth.

The radiant early morning sun shines
on the ground and through the trees
as a golden starburst appears.

It fills me with light and energy from above,
providing warmth, protection and guidance.

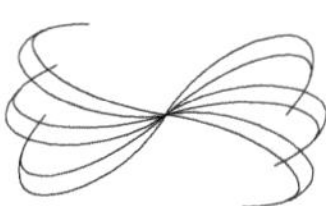

Meditation: Begin your morning sitting quietly for a few moments. Say a blessing to carry with you throughout your day. Feel the warm light of the sun as it fills you with love. Breathing in and out, feel the depth of spiritual protection, love and peace in your meditation and all through your day.

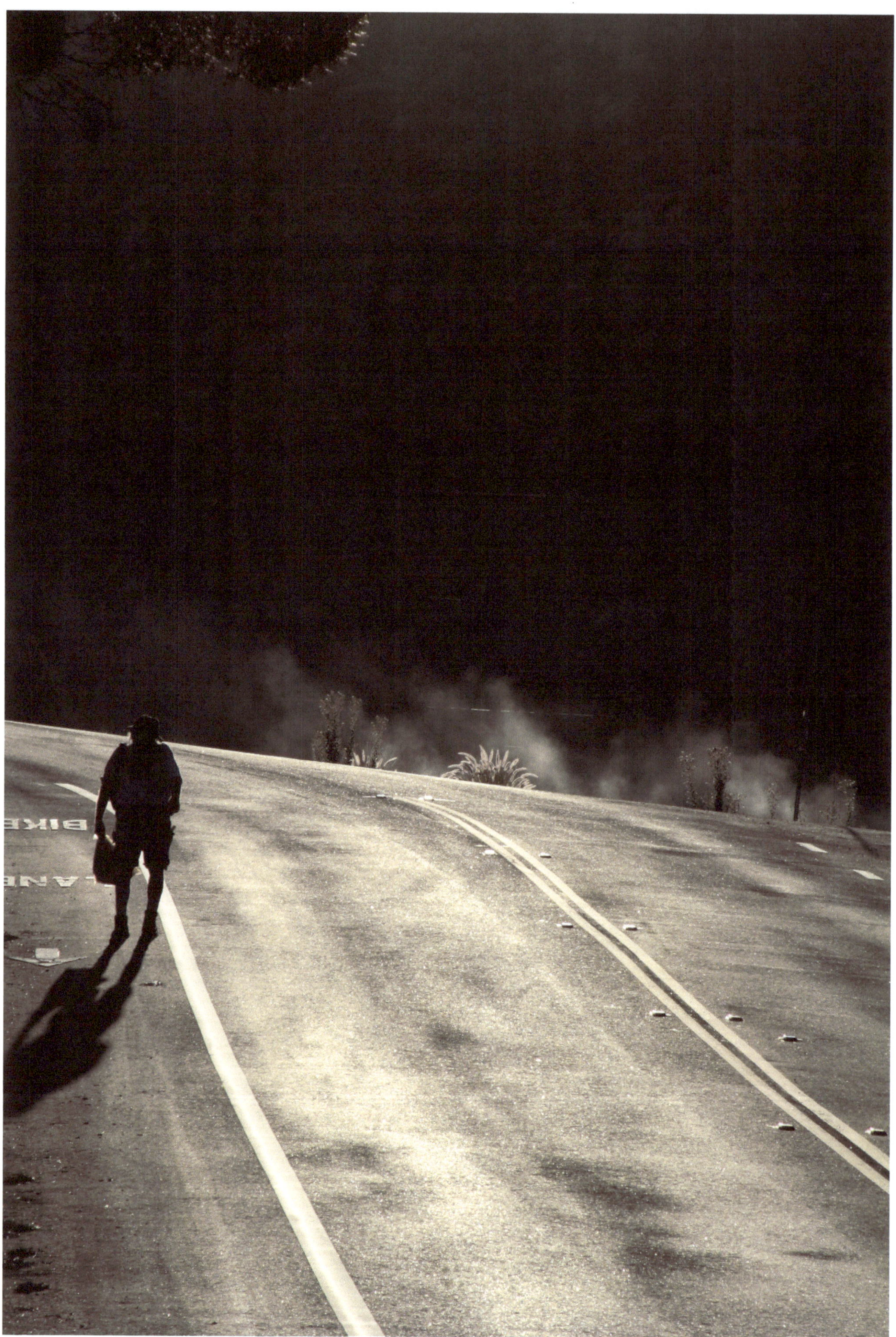

Our path in life can sometimes be lonely,

a colorless world that seems deserted and desolate

until we connect to our heart

and discover our reason for being here.

Then we awaken to the truth of who we really are

and the loneliness subsides.

Our destination and purpose becomes clear,

and we experience

peace and harmony within.

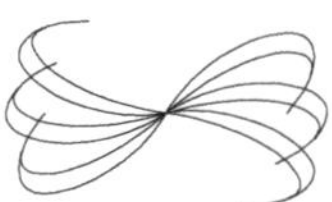

Meditation: Take a few moments to relax fully, beginning with a few deep breaths. Visualize yourself at the center of your heart. As you breathe in, imagine a bright light entering your heart, protecting you and bringing in radiant waves of love. Feel the light within and around your heart. Now, let the light expand throughout your body. Feel the loving attention you deserve. Practicing this exercise consistently will help you respect and appreciate more of who you are. It will also help you feel more love, patience and kindness for others.

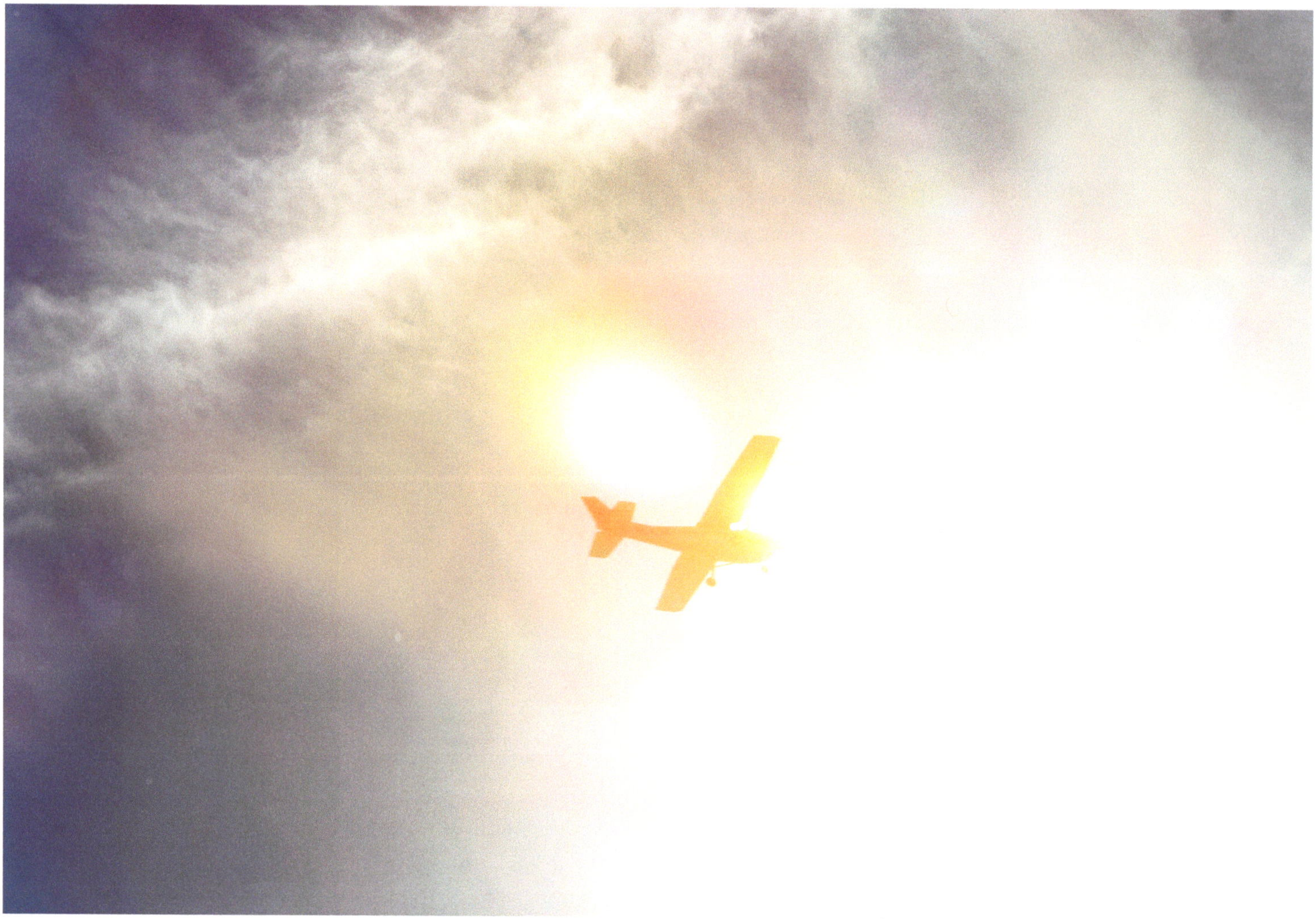

Carefree...

On a glorious day,

against the brilliant blue sky,

navigating through the billowing clouds,

the sun beaming to light the way,

flying freely.

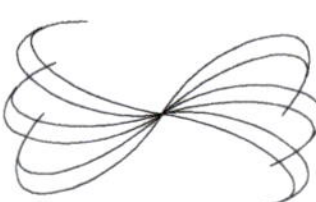

Meditation: Sitting quietly, imagine an adventure that would give you the feeling of ultimate freedom. Immerse yourself in the emotion, experiencing the sensation as though you are already enjoying freedom. Live it.

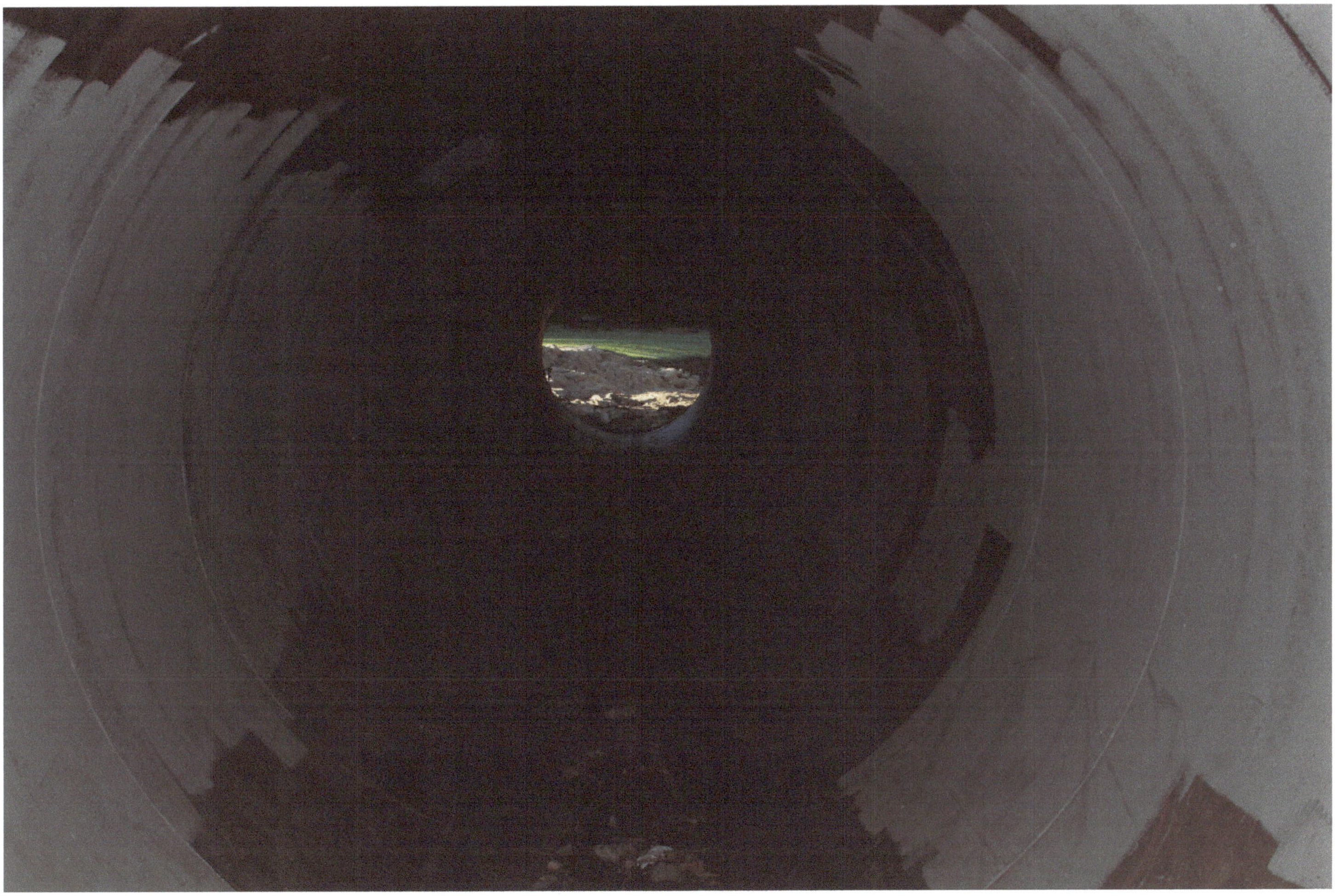

There is light at the end of the tunnel.

Green grass, sunshine and blue sky await.

Just a little further till I reach the end,

trudging through this seemingly never-ending passageway.

As I take each step,

I feel something wonderful waiting to surprise me on the other side.

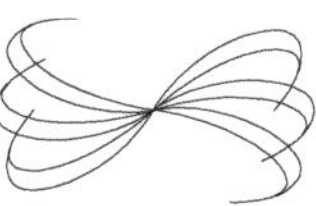

Meditation: Our jorney here is vast, enjoy all of it... pain and pleasure. Let yourself feel the power that surrounds you: the serenity, the sureness, right here and right now. As you are in this precious moment, realize there is no other time but the present.

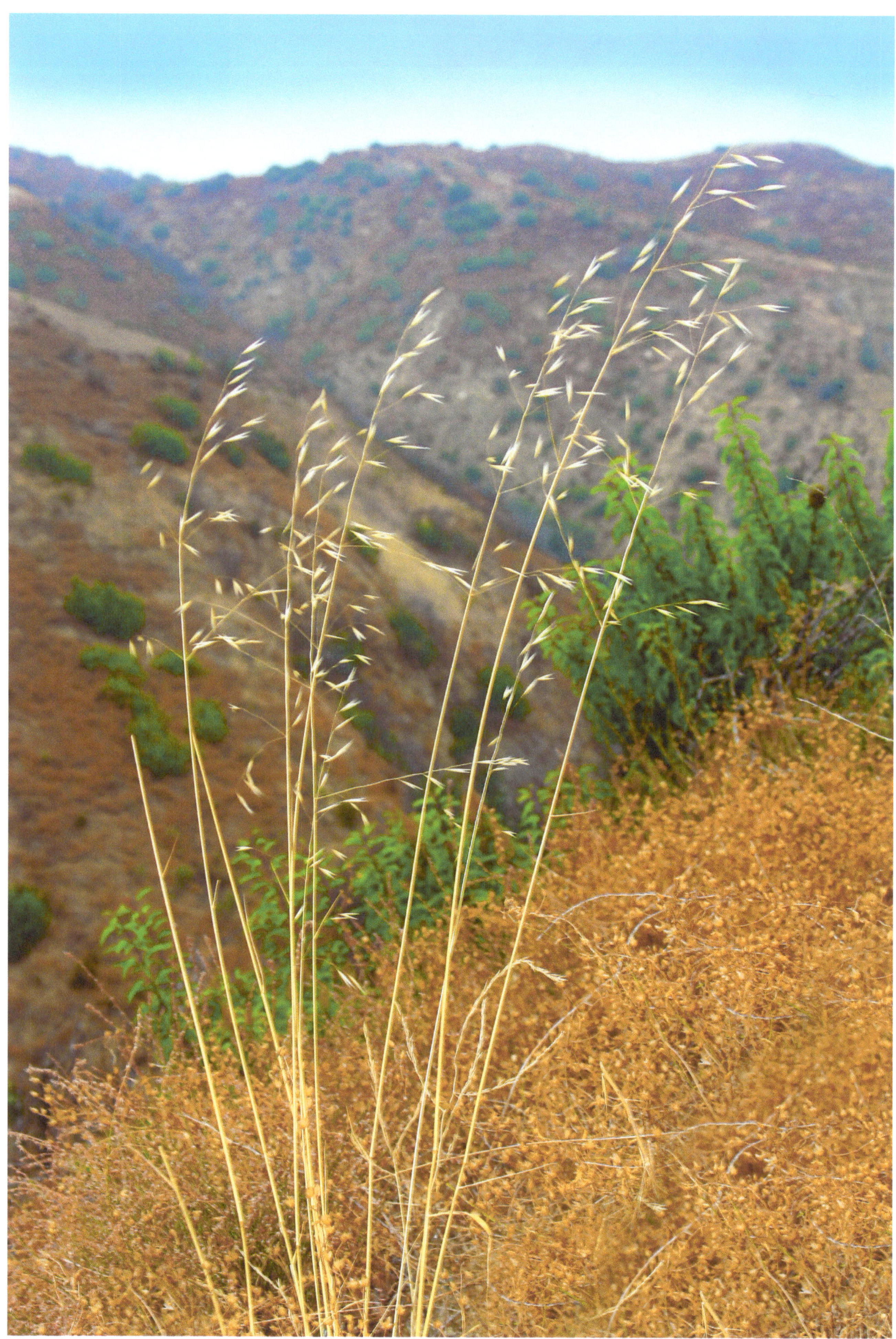

A glorious day,

keeping it simple

while feeling the gentle breeze.

It is peaceful and calming,

just blocks away from the bustling city life.

I am in my element.

I can be me

out here and carefree.

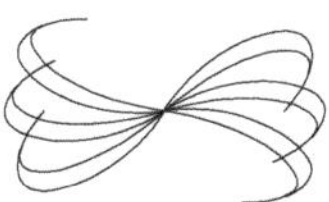

Meditation: Did you know that it's possible to feel radiance? Close your eyes and let the wind blow through your hair as you stretch and feel the air around you. It doesn't matter where you are or who is around. Feel the splendor; Feel the love of the breeze as it caresses you. Allow yourself to release the negative energy, cleansing and purifying you. Embrace it... allow it... welcome it.

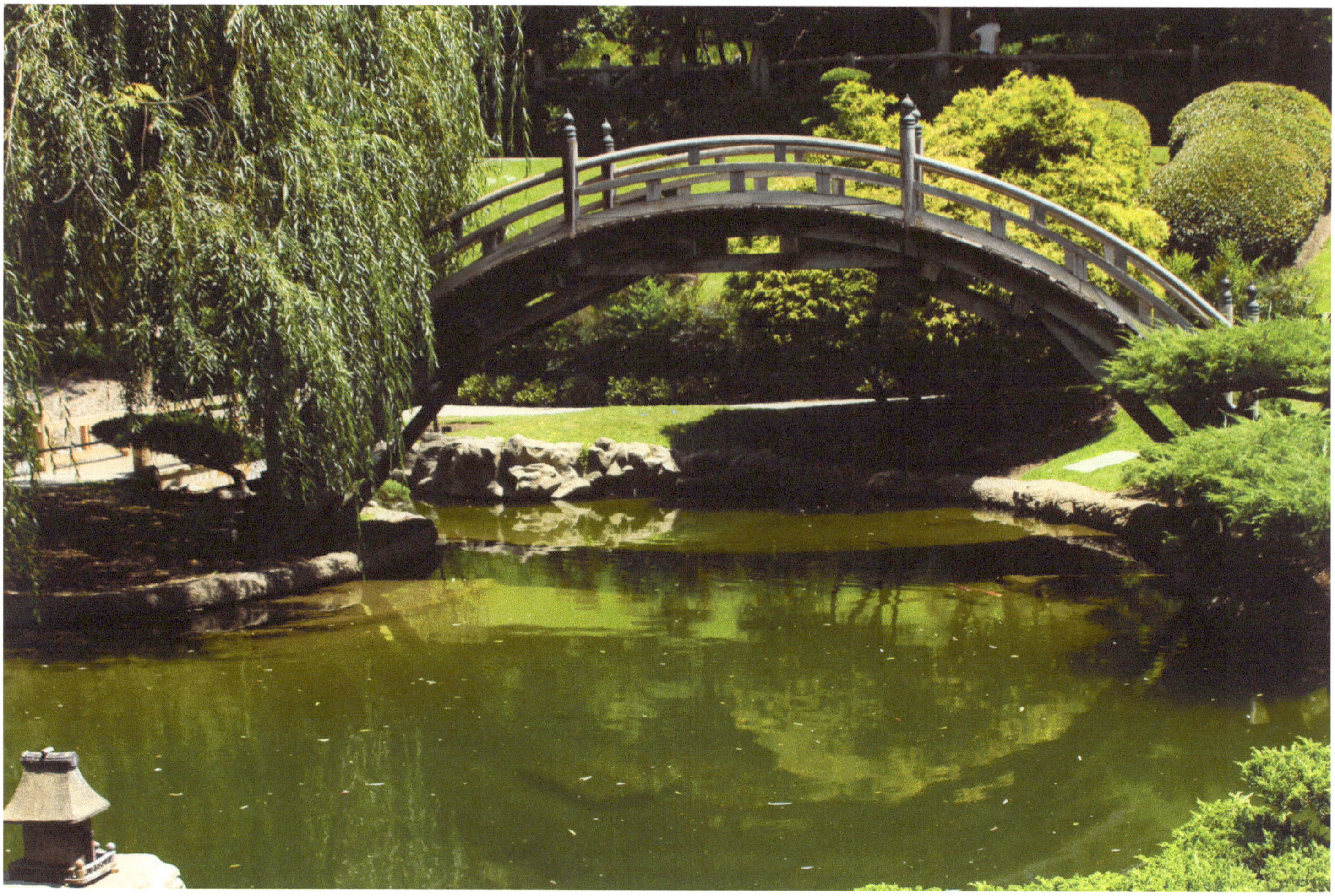

Happiness is bridged by becoming fully conscious
of our divine essence and true beauty,
then reflecting it back to others
in loving-kindness and compassion.

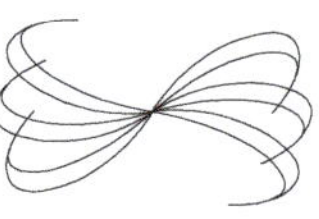

Meditation: Walking meditation cultivates mindfulness as you slow your pace to experience each step. A simple walking meditation exercise involves deliberate focusing of your attention on the sensations associated with your feet contacting the ground. If your mind begins to wander, gently bring it back and continue the practice of mindfully walking.

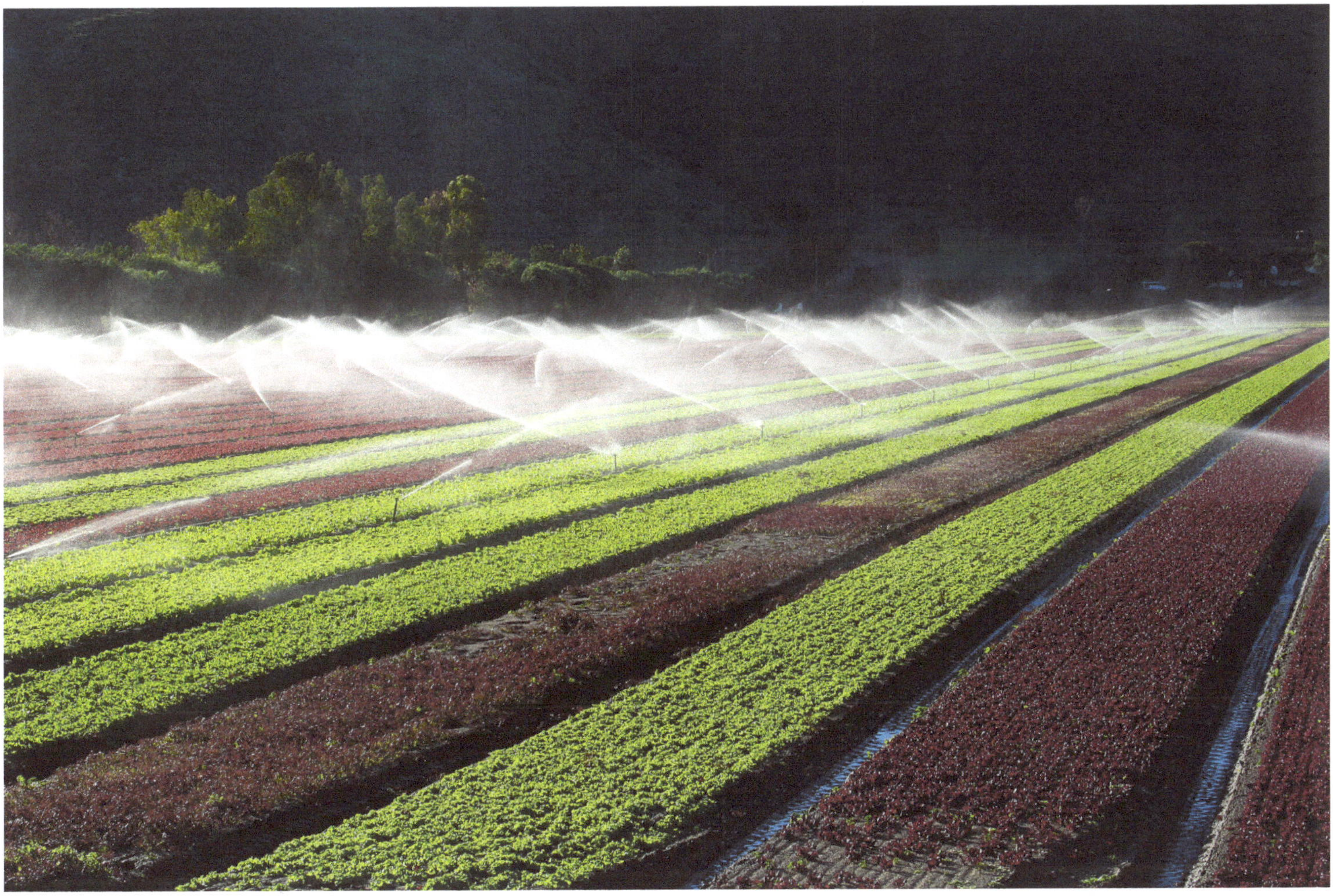

Beauty is all around us...

Awareness,

Appreciation,

Honor.

Seeing with loving eyes

as we acknowledge the gifts that surround us,

expanding our capacity to receive.

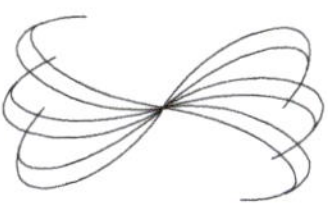

Meditation: Go within, centering yourself. Feel loving appreciation for the abundance in your life. Expand outward to your relationships, home or work environment, nature, your community, and the world. As you embrace your life from this perspective, allow yourself to feel the glory of all that is.

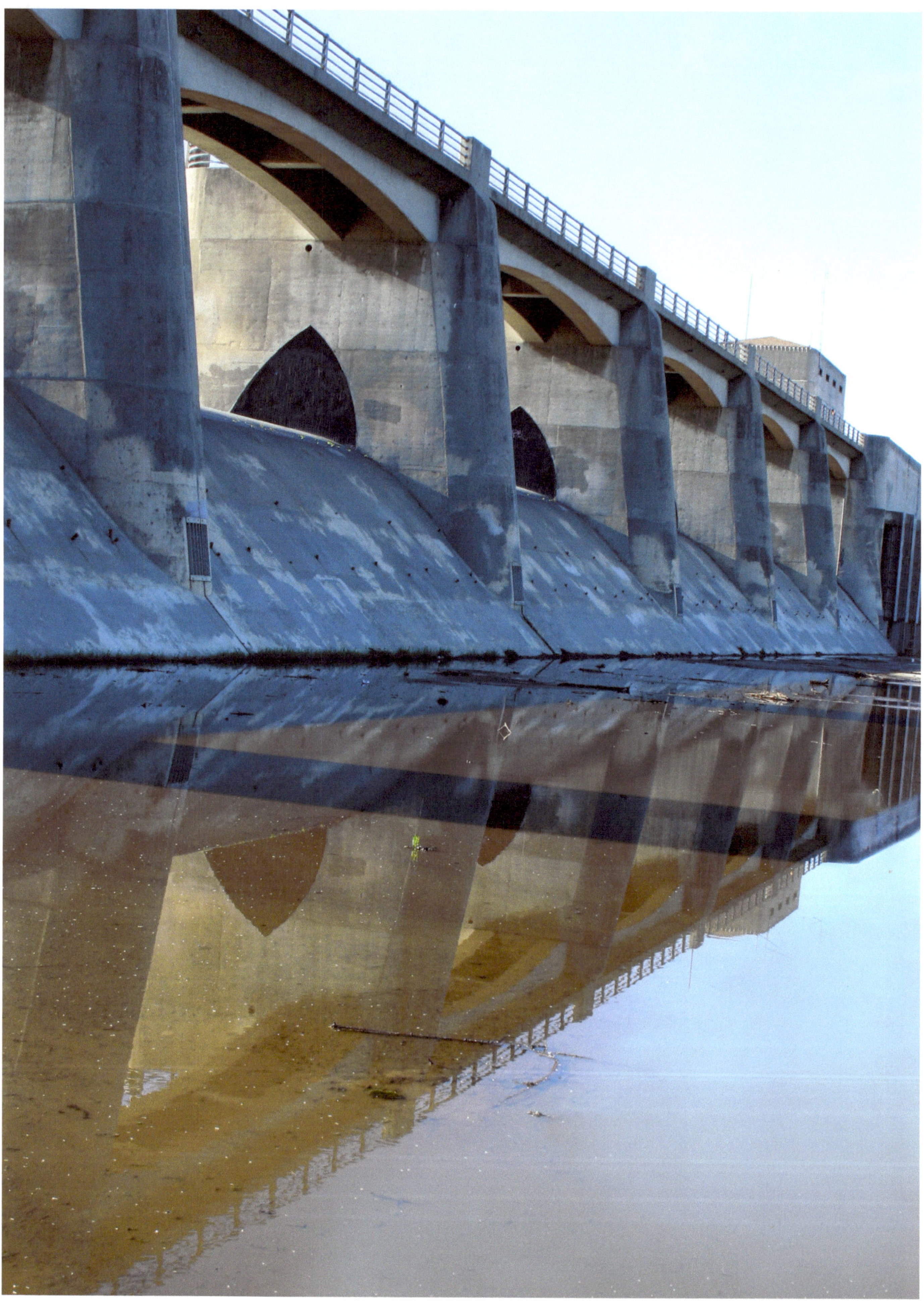

Nature's expression

in the aftermath of a rain

presents wondrous visual gifts.

Opening a creative channel enables us

to receive the joy of divine treasures

that go unnoticed in our daily existence.

Nature pauses for us to see the beauty beyond...

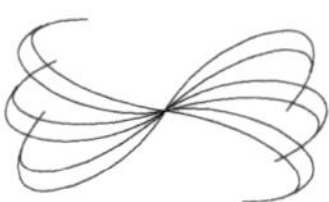

Meditation: Great things come with change. Everyone has a unique perspective on the world—developed through previous lessons and experiences. Meditation can help you be more open to alternative points of view. Start by creating a regular regimen of meditation to develop the ability to widen your perceptions. You will find a new appreciation for life that you may have missed before.

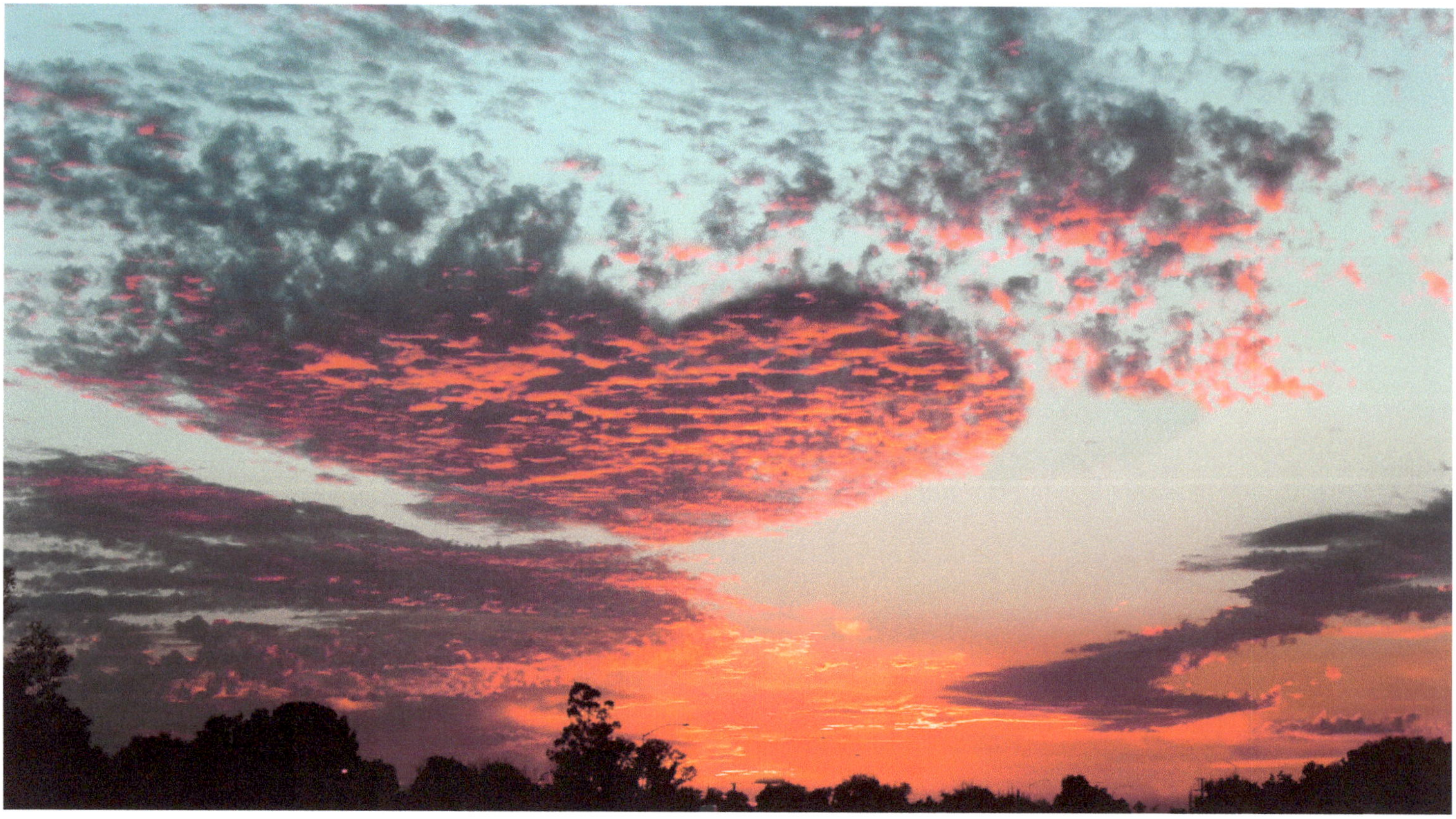

Brilliant, radiant hues
decorate the late afternoon sky
with a heartfelt message...

Love is abundant,
it is all around us.
Feel the love inside
and in all that is.

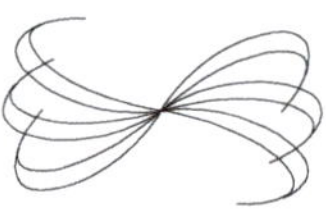

Meditation: Find something to be happy about and smile for one minute. Smiling increases the serotonin in your system and elevates your mood. Now, feel the joy and love in your heart. Carry it with you throughout your day.

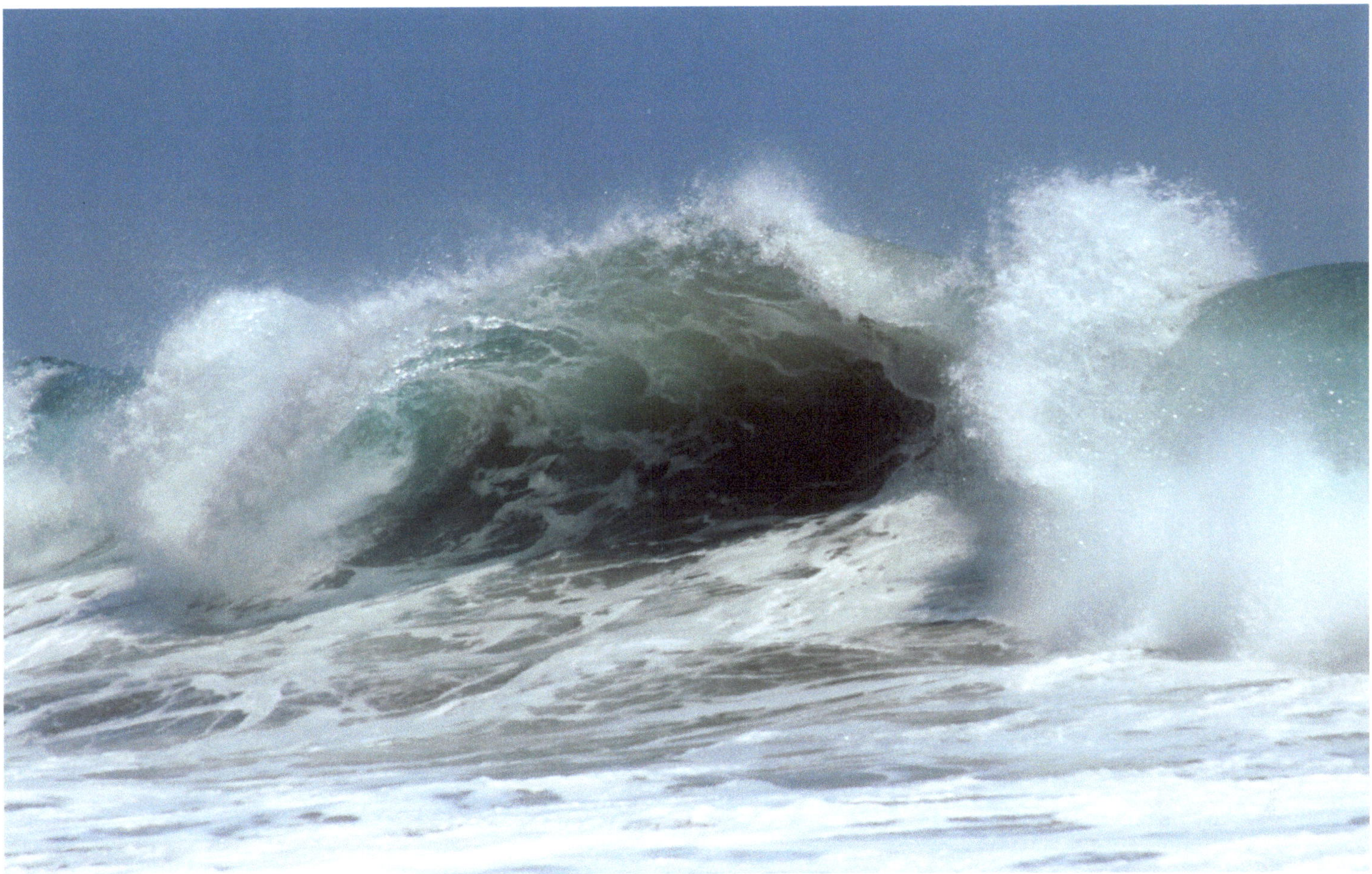

Ride the waves of your life

knowing it is easy to get caught up or dragged down.

Go with the flow,

Taking each wave as it rises.

Each one offers an extraordinary gift,

especially for you.

Feel it...

Accept it.

Ride it

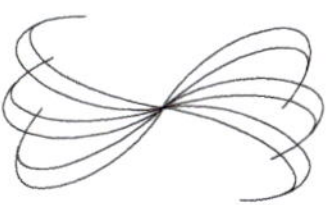

Meditation: Breathe... Feel... Accept... Allow.

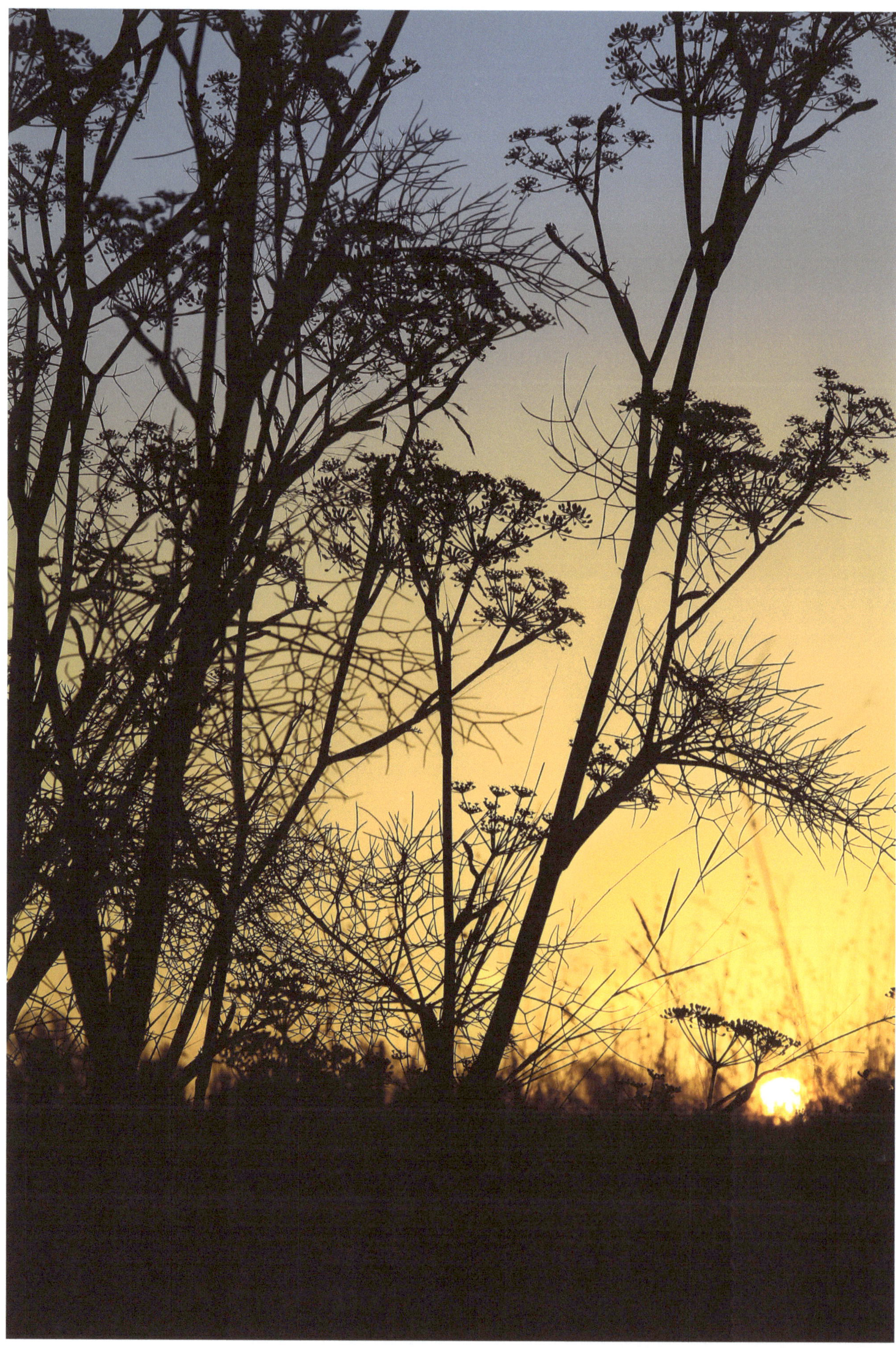

Lost in the shadows of ourselves,

hiding who we really are.

Going within to know our true self

and loving who we are unconditionally.

Be your true beauty and perfection.

Allow your light to shine.

Feel the authentic and radiant... YOU.

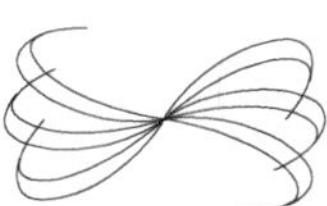

Meditation: Visualize a brilliant white light shining above your head. Allow it to flow through your body like liquid, traveling from your head to your toes creating a beautiful positive glow. Imagine it flushing out fears and negativity. As it leaves your body through the bottoms of your feet, let it ground you—connecting you to the earth. When you are ready, allow the light to surround your body and protect you. As you continue through your day or night, feel it guiding you.

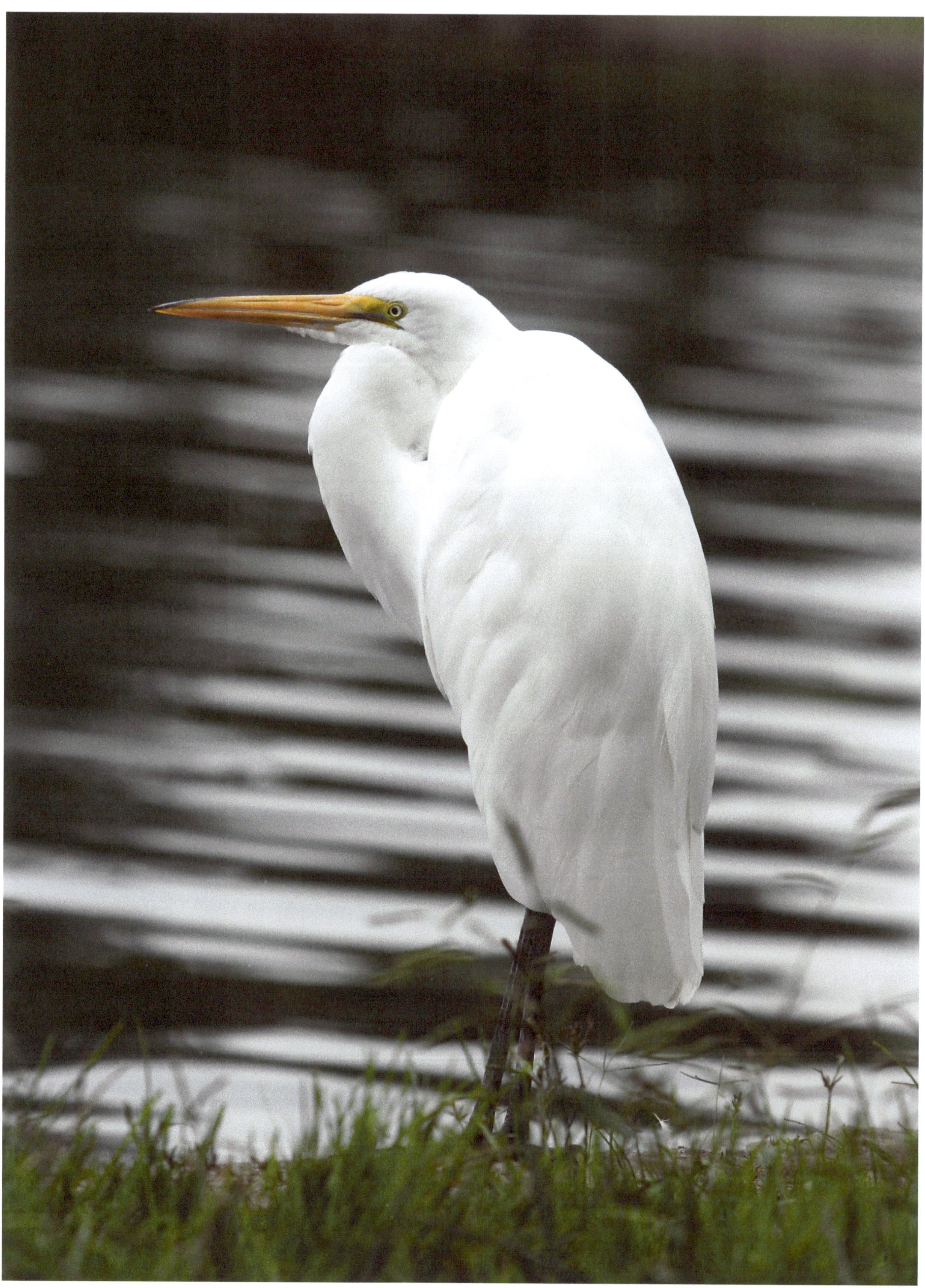

Standing on the shore,
peaceful and content,
trusting completely.
I have faith...

I know, at any moment,
I have the freedom to take flight.
I am carefree
as I take to the sky.

I am majestic and pure.
I am special.
I am beautiful.
I am unique.
I am me.

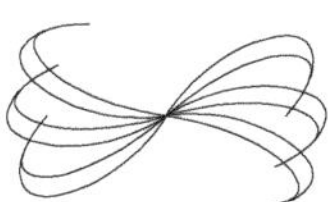

Meditation: Sit quietly in appreciation and gratitude for all that you are. Breathe in love and acceptance. Breathe out judgment, criticism, fear and doubt. You are one-of-a-kind! There will never be another you. Every one of us has extraordinary abilities and talents unlike any other. Take this realization to heart and feel your incredible preciousness. Go out and share your gifts with the world.

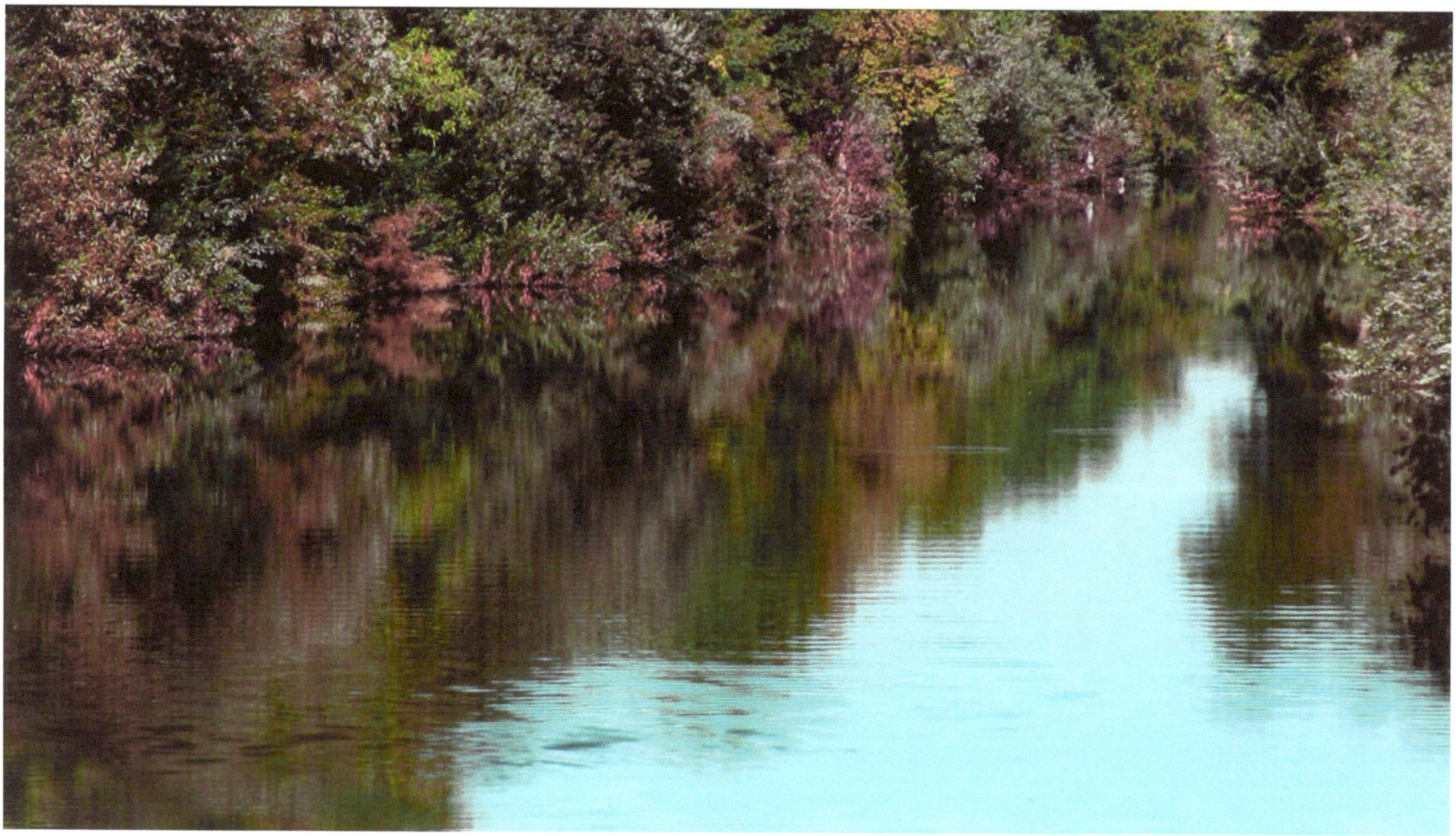

Reflections of our physical world,
mirrors our lives.
Stillness speaks volumes,
as silence is wisdom.
In peace, the universe is ours.

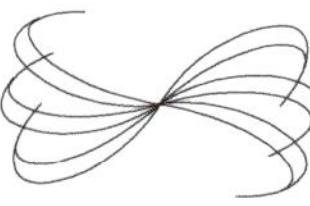

Meditation: Loving kindness is an ancient practice in which we mindfully direct loving attention into our heart, then to loved ones, and then to all beings in the world. Loving kindness meditation can be done anywhere at any time. Start by directing loving kindness toward yourself, feeling the depth of love in your heart. Now, think of those you love and extend compassion, love and peace to them. Ask that their hearts be open and happy. As you breathe more love into your heart, expand it out to the entire world.

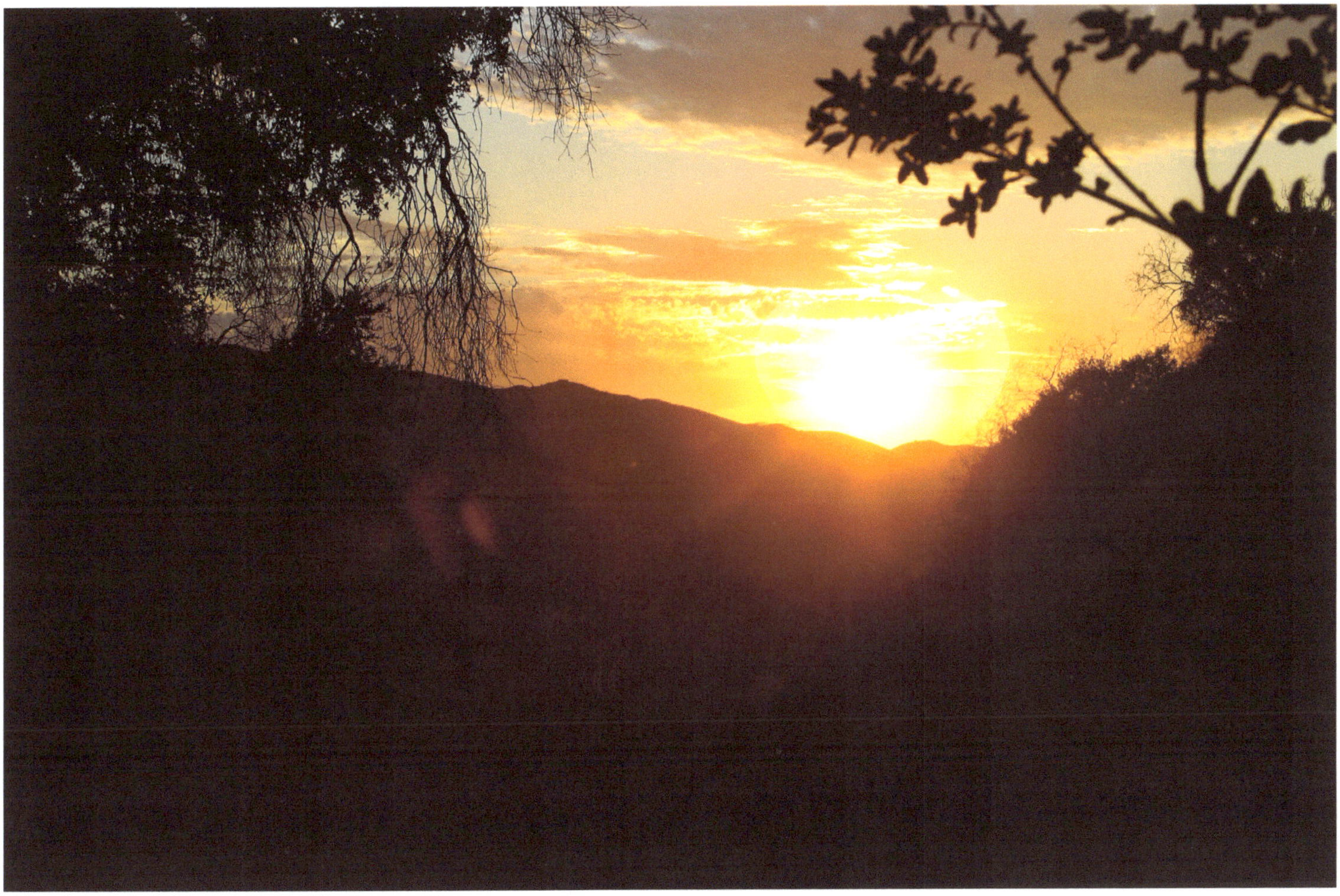

Late afternoon sun,

streaming, glowing and magnificent.

Feel the abundance of divine love

and protection surrounding us.

Balanced and aligned,

we receive the gift

of the present moment.

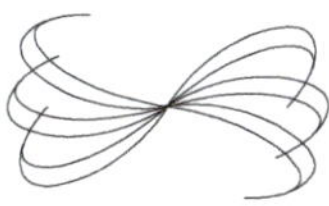

Meditation: Abundance is all around you. Take three deep, soothing breaths in through your nose and out through your mouth. Breathe in the perfect balance of all that is in the present moment. Now, tune your heart into one thing that makes you feel an overflowing of appreciation. Allow this feeling to flow freely into all areas of your life. With consistent practice, you will begin to notice that abundance is everywhere.

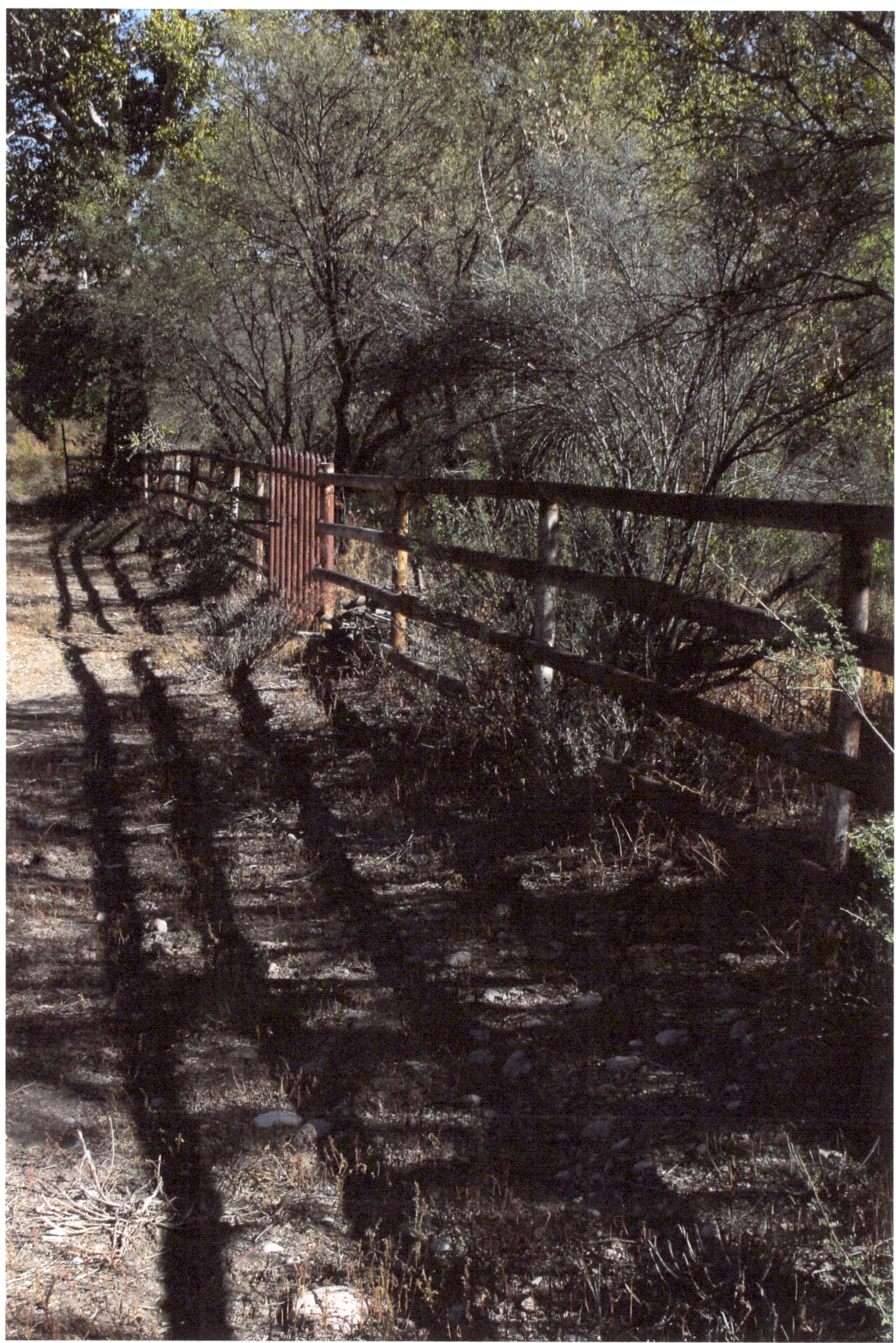

On a beautiful warm day in late October,
the desert environment is changing with the season.

Nature's beautiful imperfections,
an aged fence casting long shadows
on a carpet of fallen leaves
ready for winter.

This glorious display of nature teaches us
the ease with which it can gracefully adapt
to the changing cycles of life.

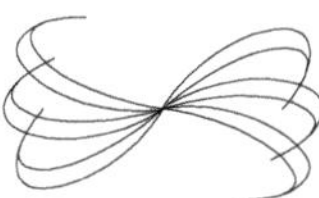

Meditation: When you have an opportunity to experience something for the first time, you do so with a beginner's mind. When you experience something for a second, third or hundredth time, try to give it the same level of attention and presence that you did the first time. Can you apply a beginner's mind to all that you do? Be mindful of opportunities to look at the world with a fresh pair of eyes. You will see things you never saw before.

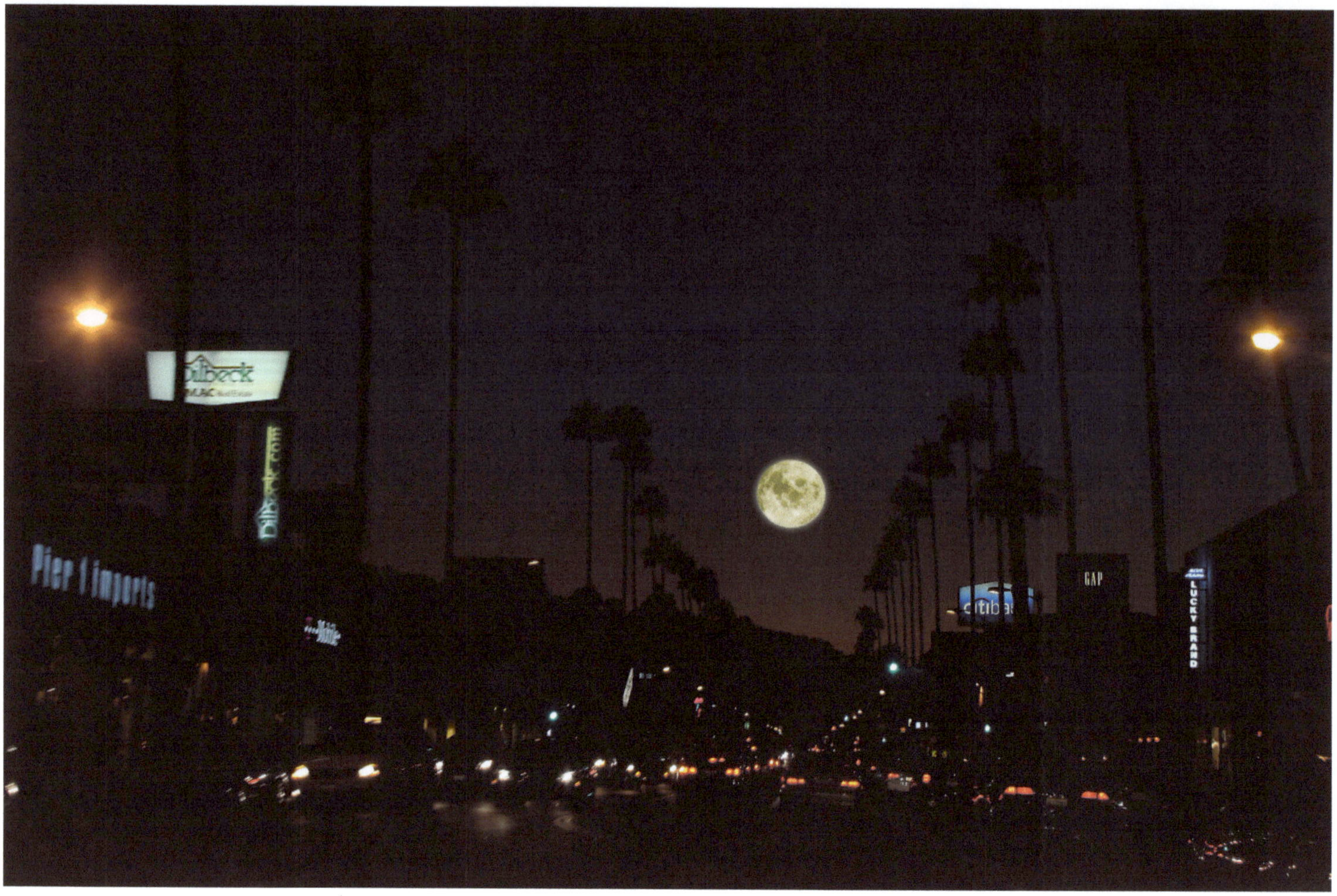

The spirit of the night.

The contrast of the lively city.

The magical skyscape,

bigger than life.

Majestic,

energetic,

and awe-inspiring.

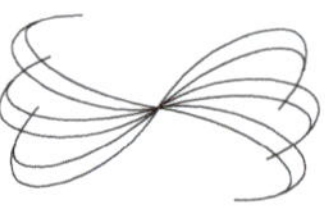

Meditation: We are the source of our own happiness—though life polarizes our actions and experiences: black and white, light and dark, positive and negative. When we understand our responsibility to achieve the sense of harmony, well-being and fulfillment we desire, we can live a richer life. In every moment, we have a choice. If we experience what we perceive as unpleasant, it is our responsibility to change and view life from a positive perspective. When we harmonize our thoughts, beliefs and actions, we can find profound inner peace and prosperity.

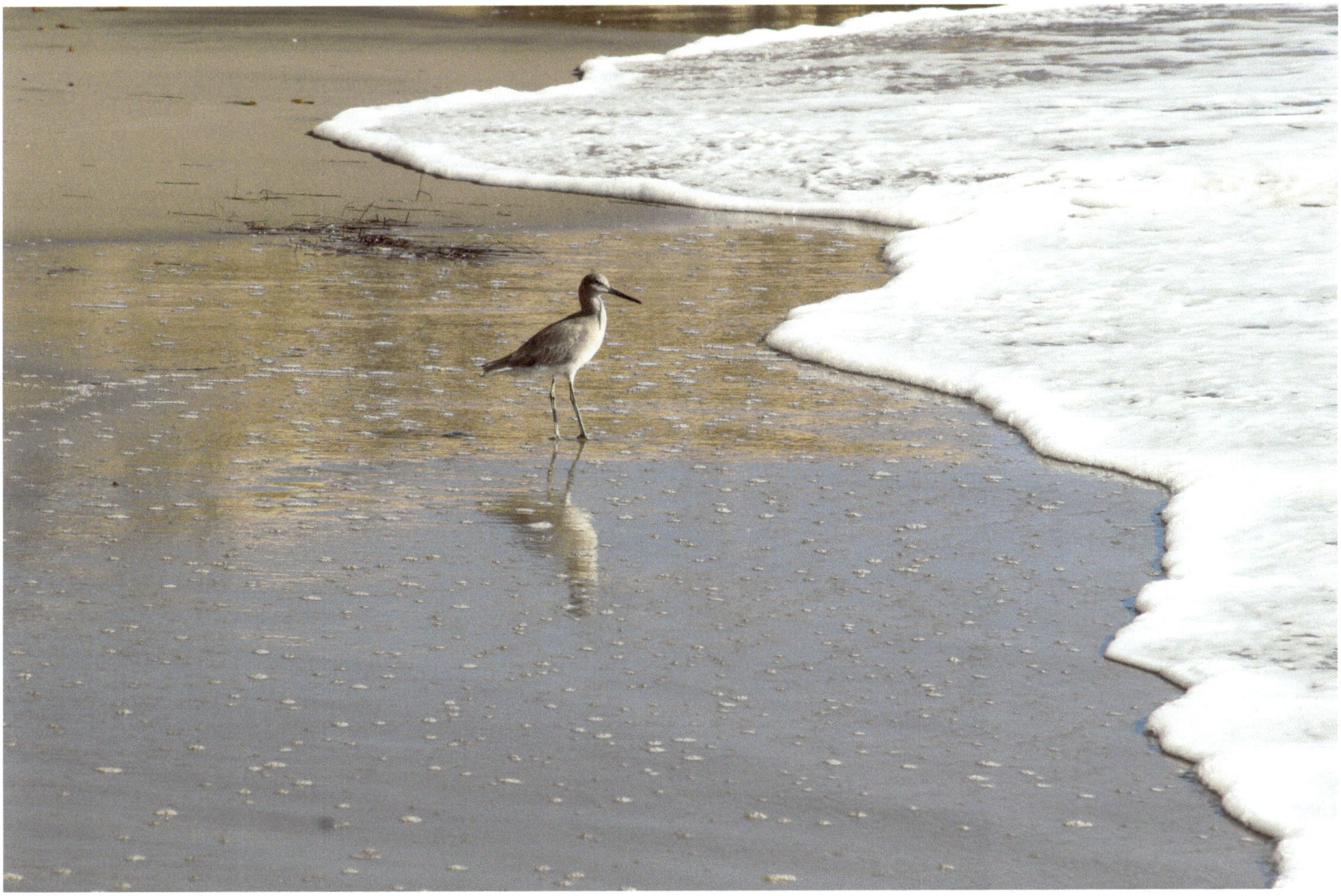

Enjoying alone time,
loving who I am.
There is no need for anyone
or anything else in this moment.
What a glorious way to be.
I am not alone,
my loving reflection is here with me,
and sometimes this is all that is necessary.

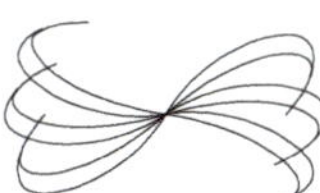

Meditation: Walk around in your bare feet. Connect with the earth beneath you. Feel the pure life-force and radiating energy. Walk on different natural surfaces: sand, grass, soil or shallow water. Become one with nature's elements as you ground to Mother Earth.

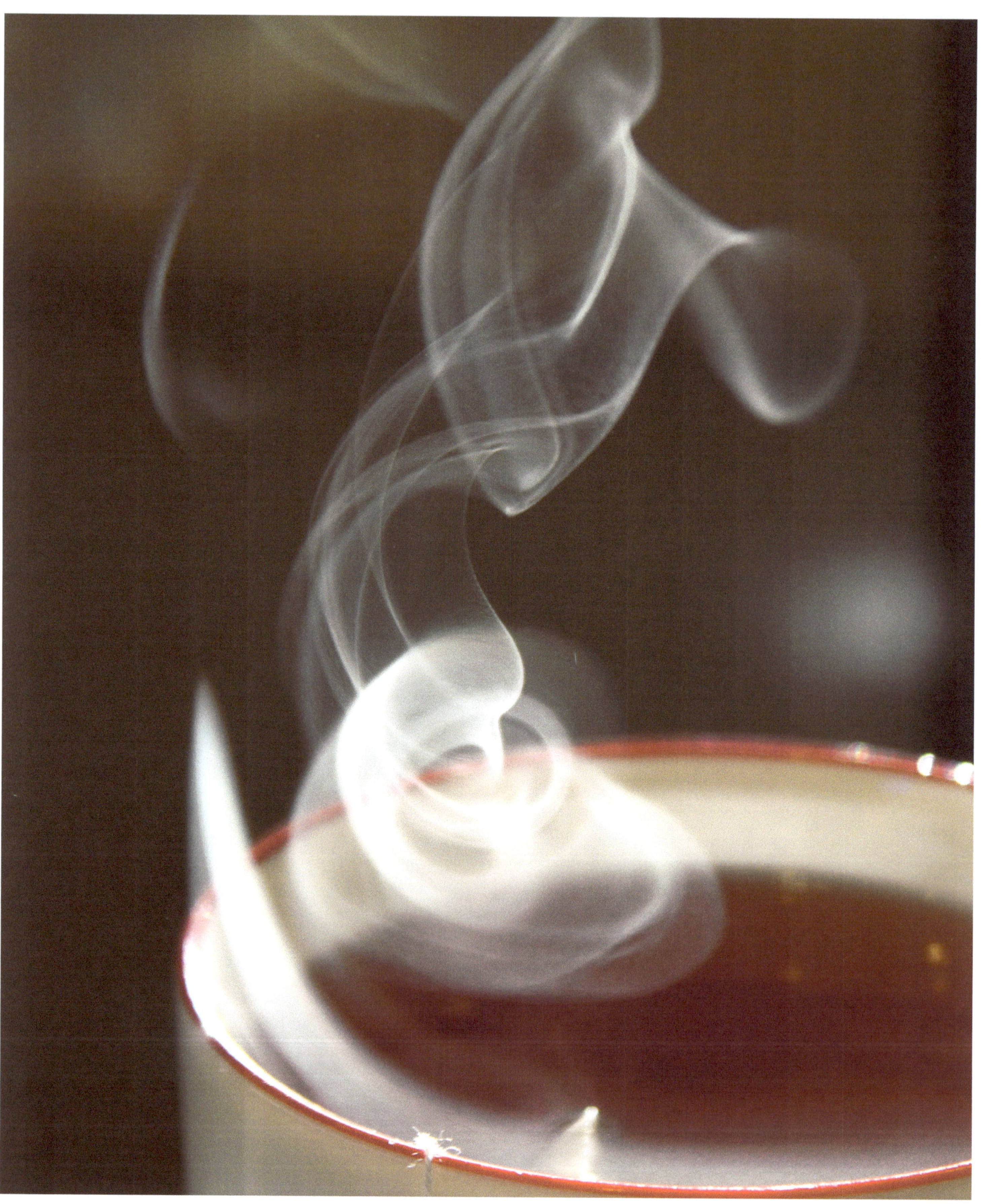

Sun streams through the window

as hearts swirl and rise,

full of love,

warmth,

and protection.

An angel appears,

a radiant being of love,

a guiding light.

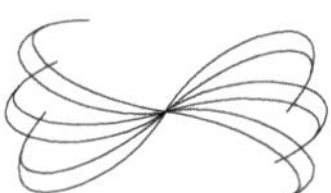

Meditation: The universe provides you with clues to help you move through life with ease. It's easy to miss them if you aren't fully aware. Keep a journal of these occurrences. Is there a pattern, something symbolic, or a recurring message? This indicates someone or something is guiding you with wisdom that is always available. It will come to you through a higher state of awareness. Ask for guidance and allow the clear messages to come through.

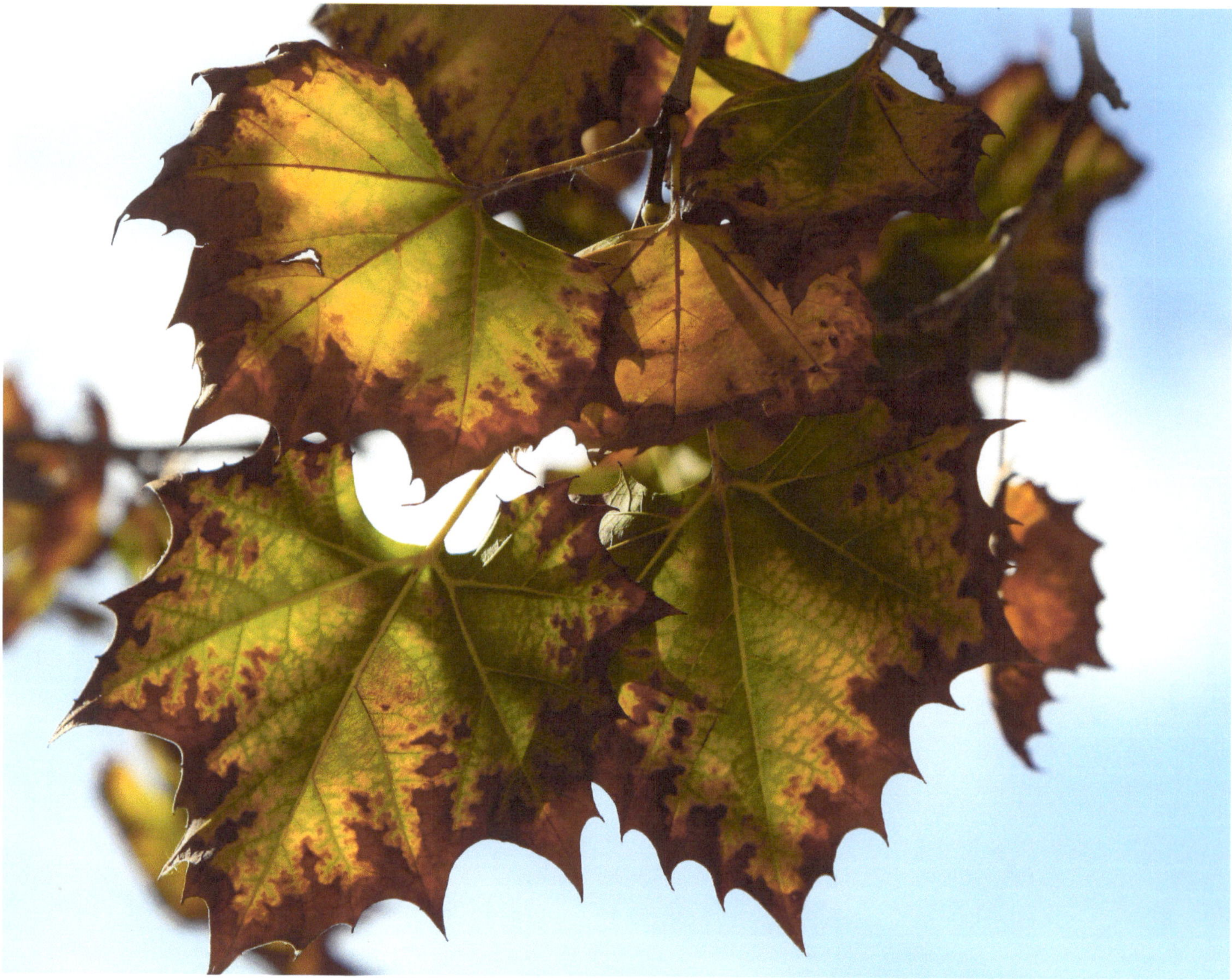

Freedom...

Autumn bursts into a colorful finale

as though nature has been saving up all year.

Every leaf is in harmony with the magic of the season,

glowing expressions of transformation.

Divine perfection

in all its glory.

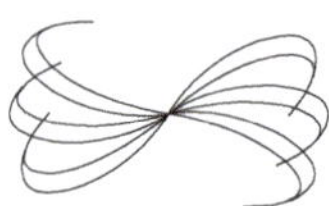

Meditation: Life at this time of transformation is a tremendous gift. Everything that happens is there to teach you and help you grow into the best version of your Self. Your job is to accept your ever-changing life unconditionally, allowing it to flow with ease and grace. Take some time to journal about the ways in which your life is unfolding with meaning and purpose. Remember to acknowledge the beauty in the transformation that takes place every day.

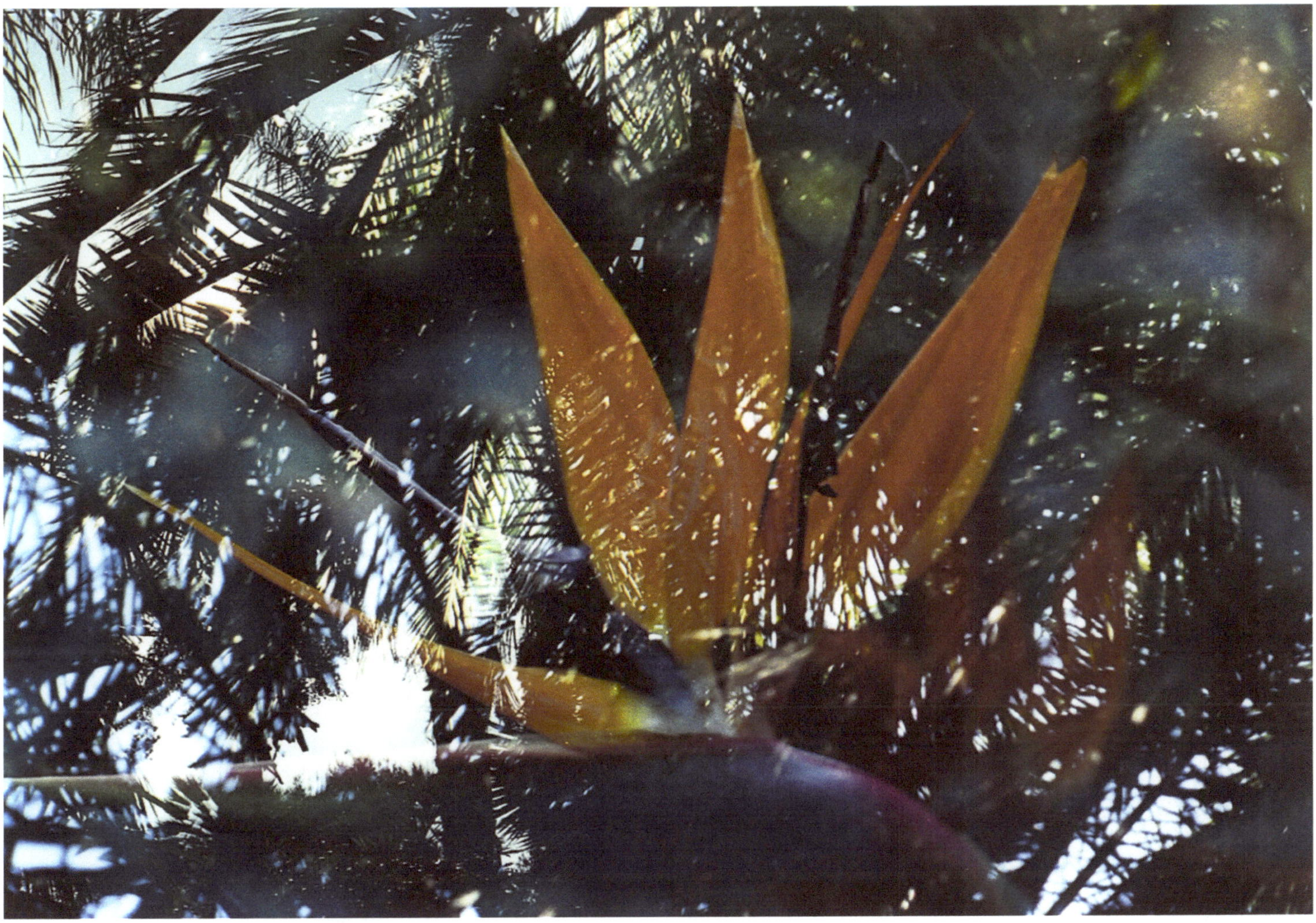

Synchronicities

whispering to our soul,

"Everything happens for a reason."

Seemingly accidental,

beautiful coincidences.

Acceptance...

Receiving...

Learning...

Signs of spiritual awakening.

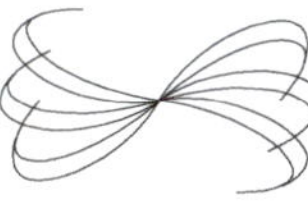

Meditation: How often do you recognize when you are in the right place at the right time? The more you pay attention to these scenarios, the more often they will occur. The universe is telling you something. Keep a log or journal of the synchronicities that happen every day. You will find they are meant to be. Take a closer look through meditation and allow yourself to ponder the meanings of these events. What are they telling you?

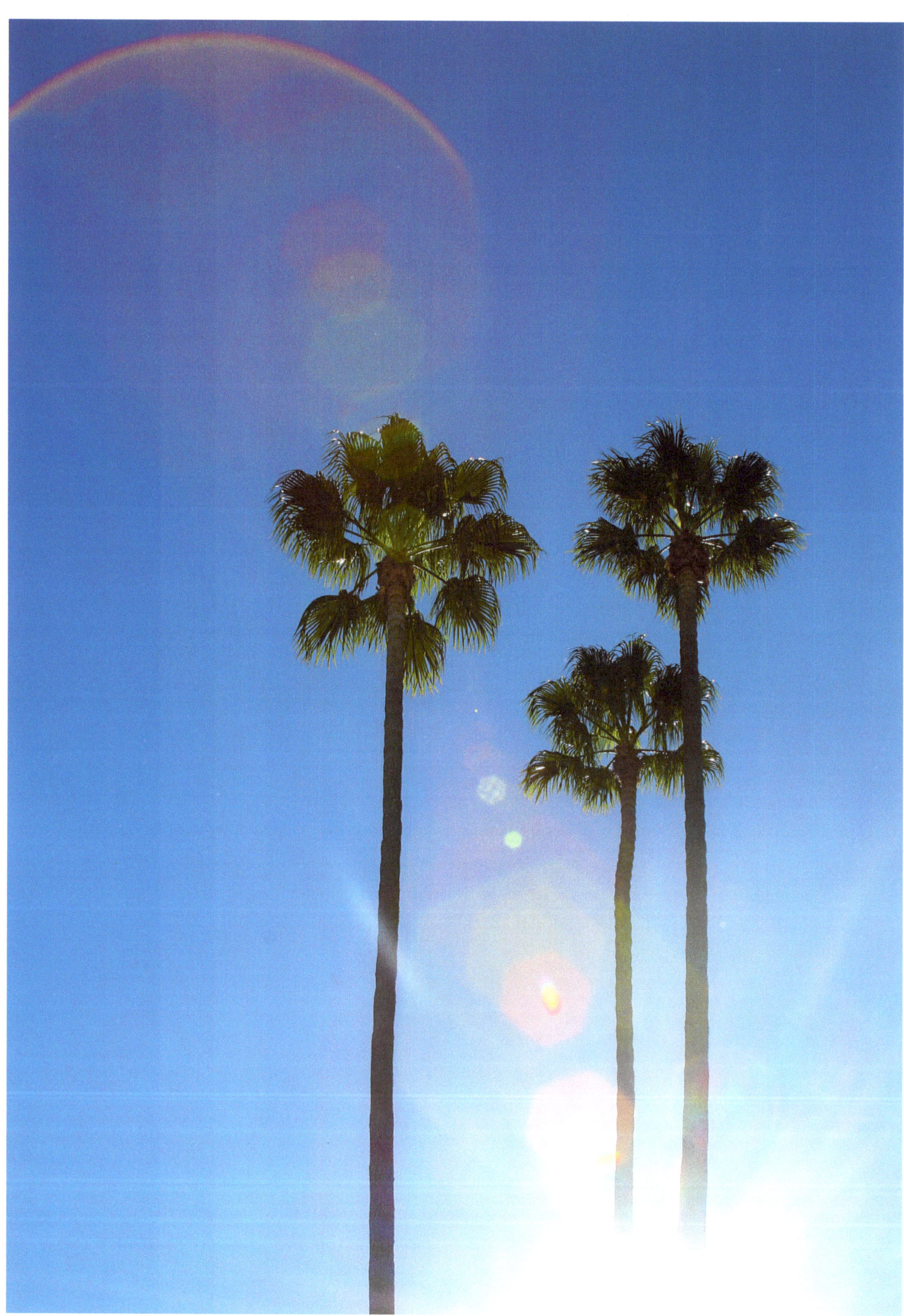

Three palms stood tall and proud,

bathing in the early morning sun.

Refractions of light,

glowing in perfection

against the brilliant blue sky.

Impressive...

Graceful...

Majestic...

Radiating energy

to the heavens.

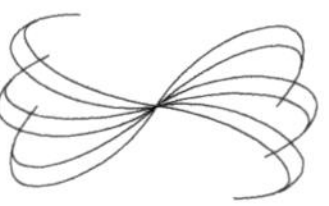

Meditation: No matter where you are, what you are doing, or how hectic things become... Slow down. Pick a time in your day when you are able to be 100 percent present—without any distractions. Tune into your amazing senses, allowing yourself to experience taste, touch, aroma, sight and sound. What do you notice? Can you come closer to the full experience? What is it telling you? What emotion accompanies it? When you are completely present with your extraordinary senses, you will experience wonderful surprises.

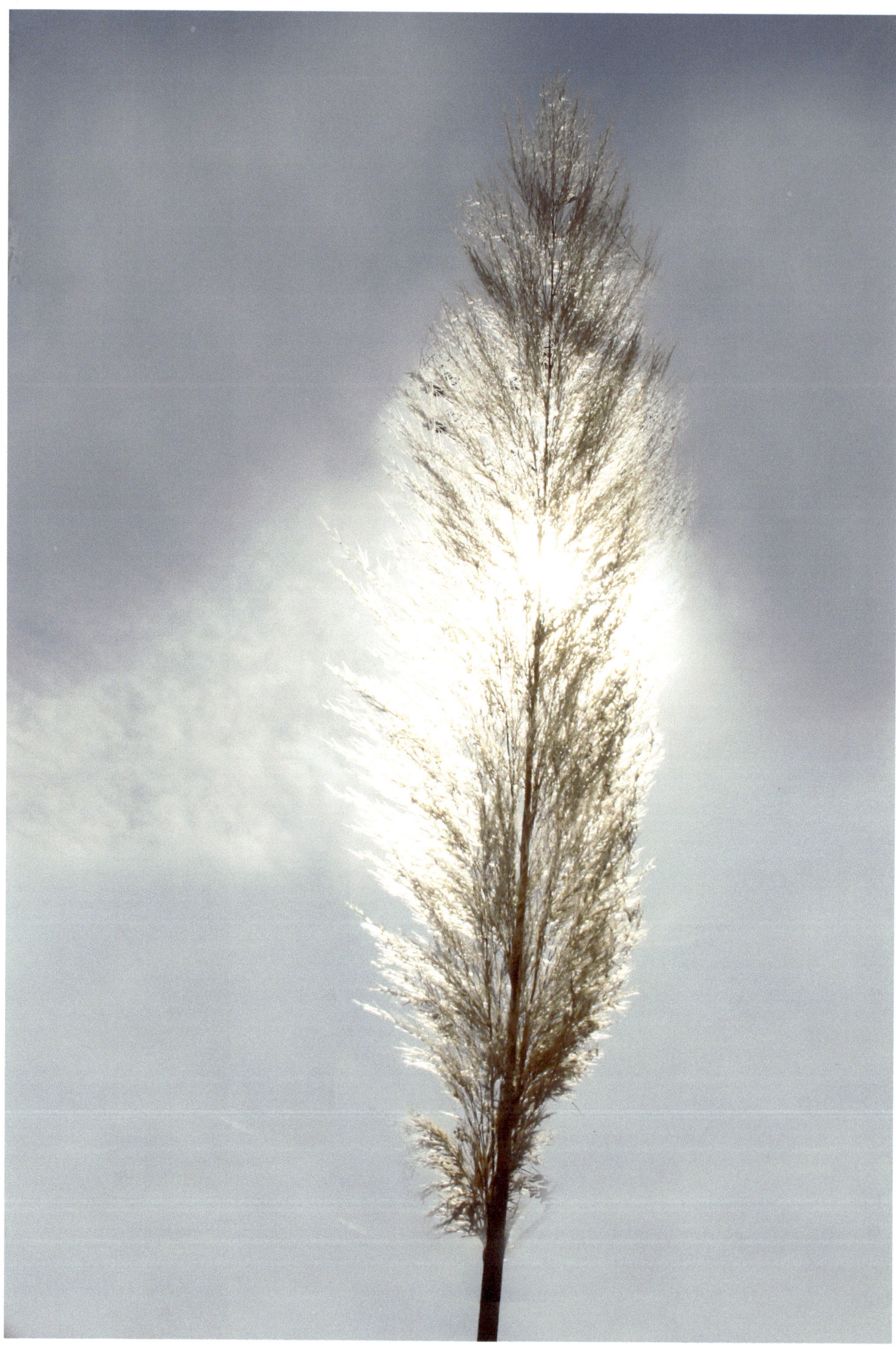

Thank you, Mother Earth,
for providing rich soil to grow,
sunlight to nurture,
rainwater to sustain.
You give us nourishment
for all we need to grow and thrive,
to stay healthy,
without expecting anything in return.

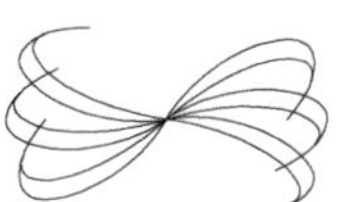

Meditation: You can do much good for the world on an individual level. Go into your heart and visualize a planet where everyone can appreciate and respect all it provides. Imagine a place where everyone feels love and honor for one another. Allow this deep love to extend out to the resources you receive from Mother Earth. Now, imagine our earth as a clean, healthy, peaceful place where we can all feel safe and loved. As you do more of this type of meditation, you affect the global consciousness of the planet and create change.

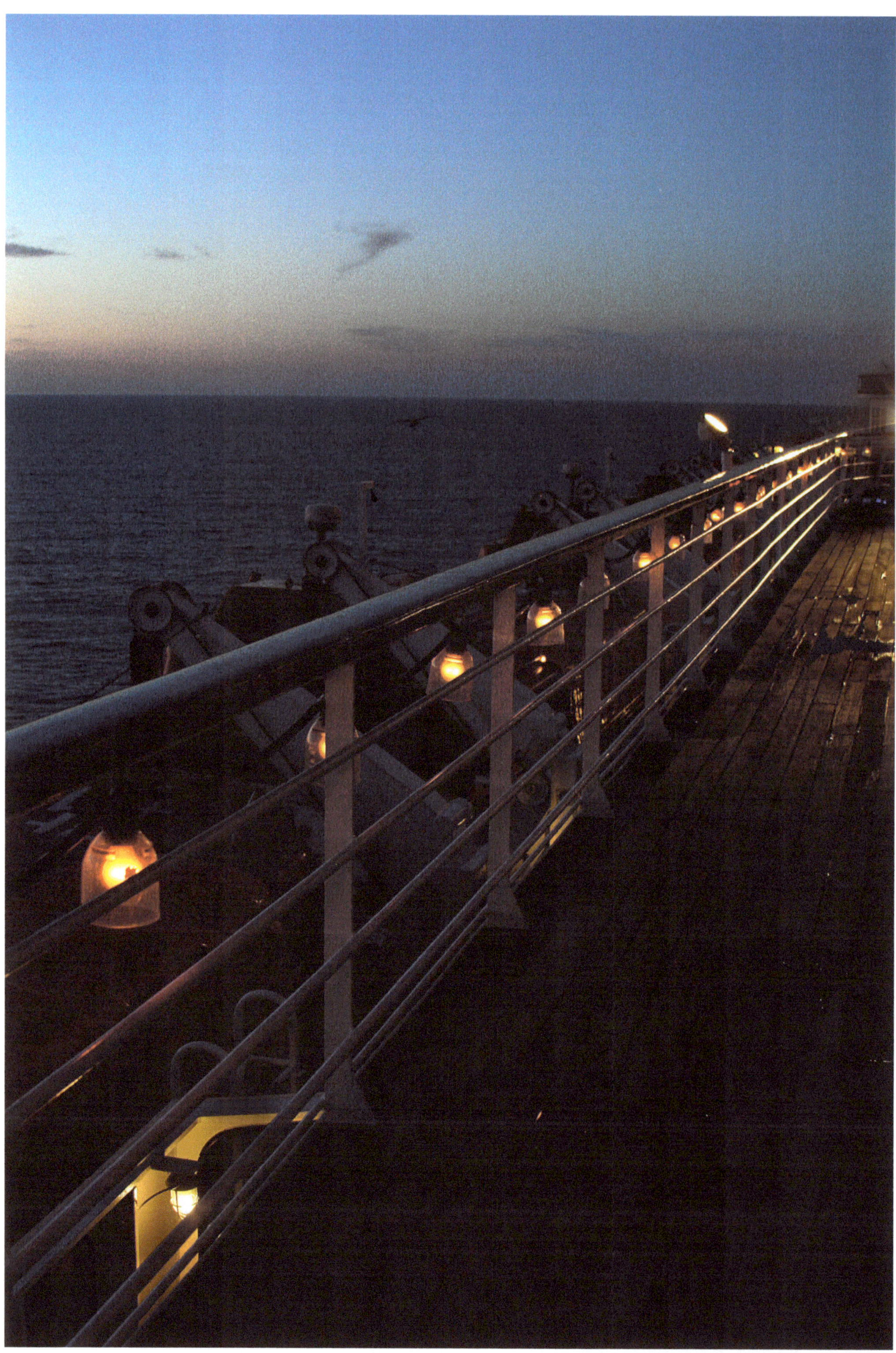

Dusk moves in.

Day turns to night.

Luminous moods accentuate

twilight vision,

an appreciation of all that is.

A bird flies by.

Little puddles of water

sparkle in the lights.

Breathe in tranquility

moment by moment.

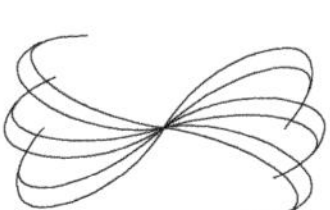

Meditation: Great treasures come from the heart. The more you share your treasures with others, the more you receive in return. Prosperity always starts with you. When you give more love, you receive more love—and more patience, compassion and forgiveness. Open your mind and heart to feel this love from within before extending it outward.

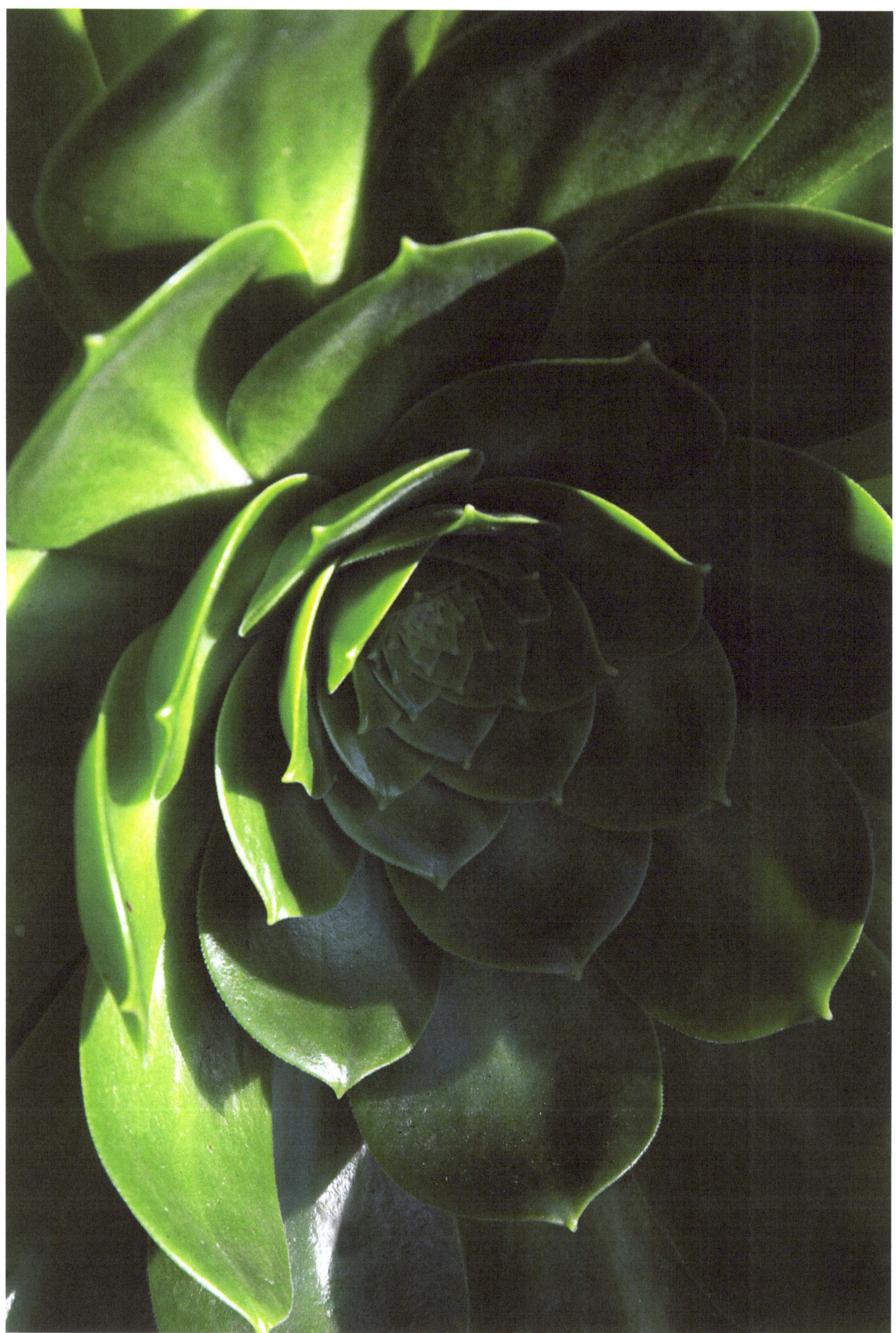

Blessed by the gifts of the universe,

here to grow and thrive.

Radiant and robust,

hearty and bountiful,

naturally harmonious,

effortless grace

in divine perfection.

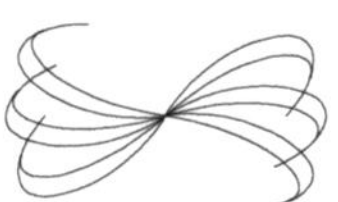

Meditation: Nature is effortless and spontaneous. If you observe nature at work, you will clearly see that little effort is expended. Grass doesn't try to grow, it just grows. Flowers don't try to bloom, they just bloom. It is the nature of the sun to shine. You were also born to grow and thrive effortlessly. Sit quietly, letting go of the "wanting mind." You don't need to struggle to fulfill your desires. Sit patiently with effortless ease, allowing things to come in the right moment. Wait for the perfect season for your desires to blossom into reality.

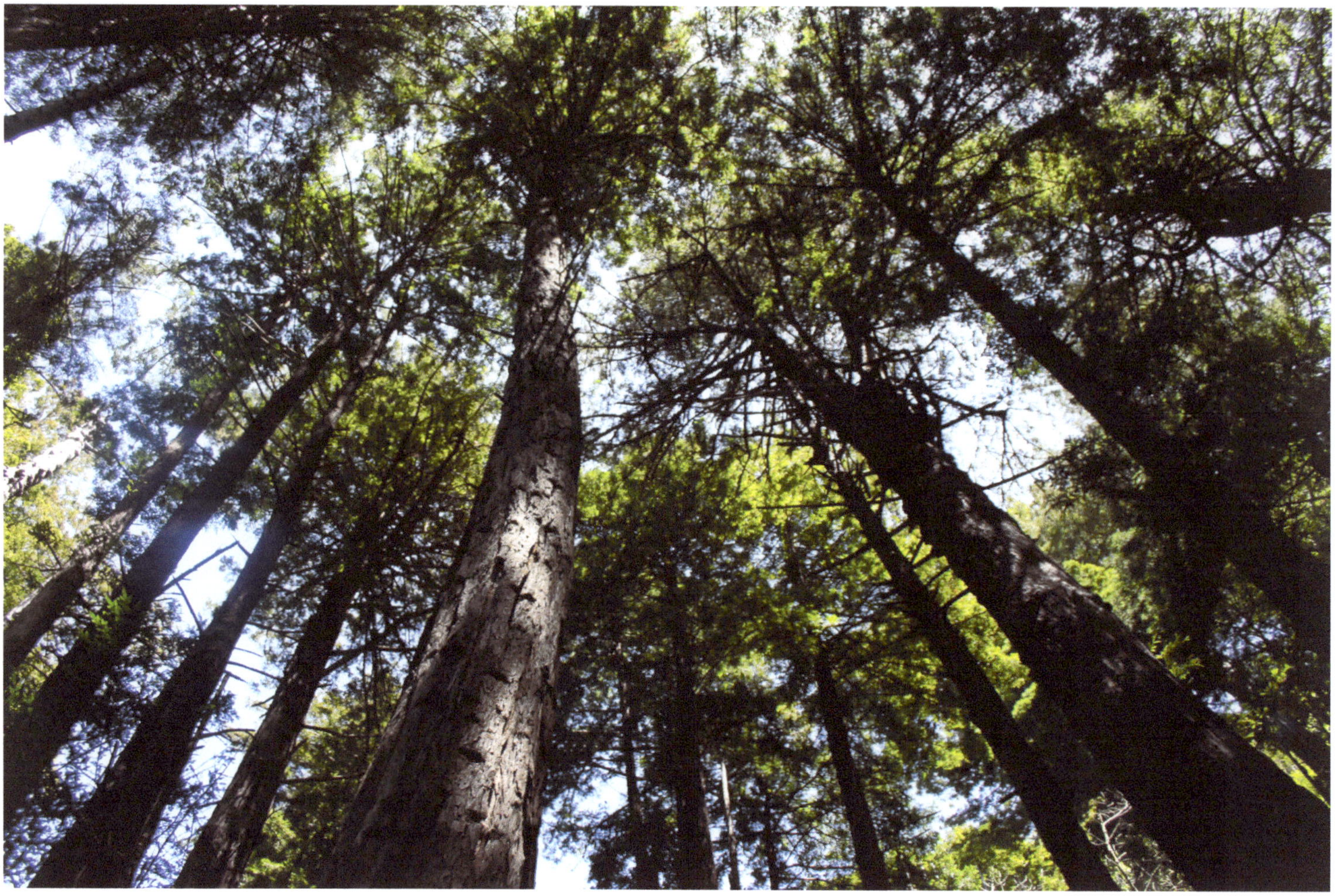

Behold the power of the Universe.

Beautiful in peace,

wise in silence,

each perfect in their own way.

Witness the strength of the mighty sequoias

standing in unity.

They are one

just as we are.

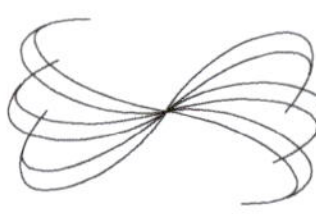

Meditation: Take a moment to sit quietly. Breathe deeply into your heart, filling it with love. Smile as you release your breath—purging tension, stress and fear from your body. Now take in a deeper breath of love. As you breathe out, visualize expanding your positive loving energy out to the universe. Repeat this exercise several times whenever you feel fear, stress or tension. There is loving energy in your heart and peace is always a breath away. Namasté.

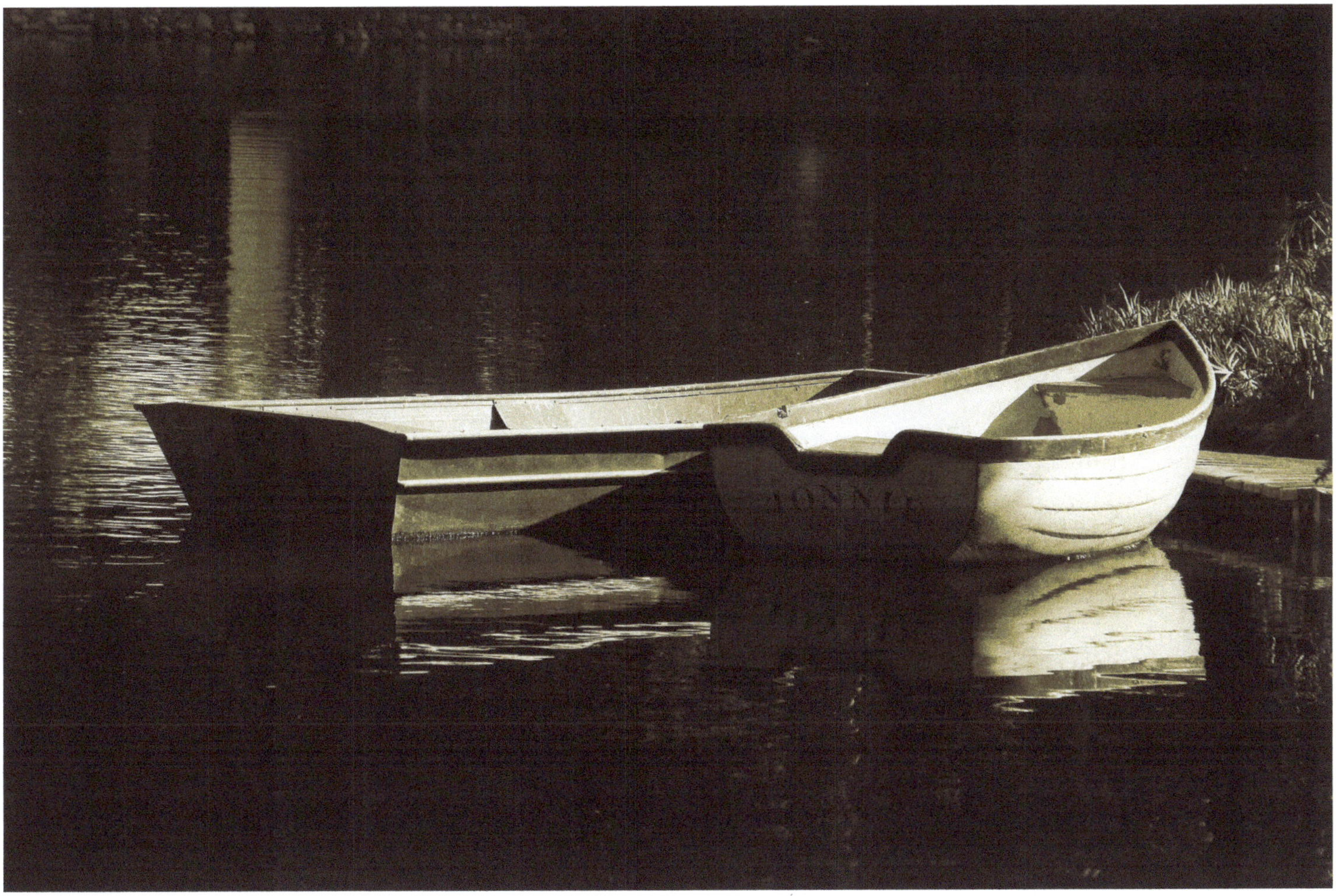

Peacefulness plays
on the calm, still water.
We are present,
resting together.
Nothing needs to be said
as we soak up the wonder
and deep appreciation
of the simplicity.

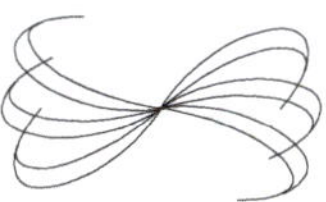

Meditation: Allow yourself to sit with everything that is. There is nowhere you need to be and nothing that you need to do. Just be present with all that is in this moment. Say to yourself, "I am exactly where I am supposed to be, and I am perfect, just as I am." It's that simple!

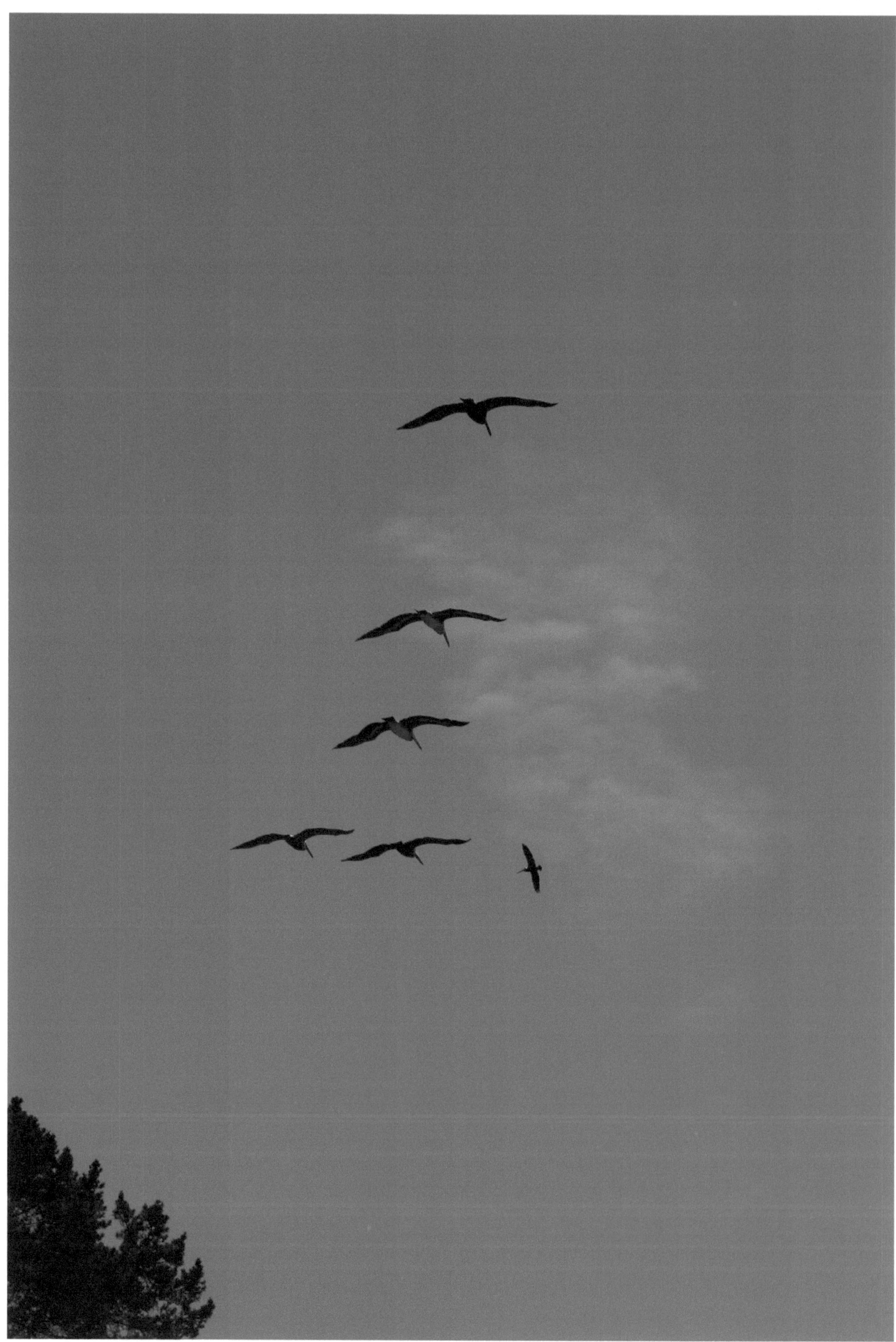

Lifetimes of disharmony

sway us away from honoring our heart.

The true path lies within.

Each unto its own,

individual...

unique...

personal...

soaring freely

without boundaries,

courageous and valiant.

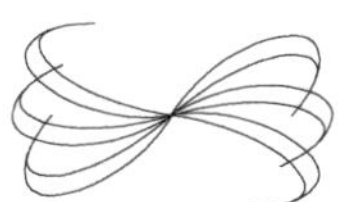

Meditation: Listen to your heart, it always knows. What is it that you really desire? Tune out the chatter in your mind as you breathe into your heart, tapping into your inner wisdom and listening intently to what comes through. This is your true desire. Ask yourself... Does this feel good? In this moment, you are accessing your higher consciousness—your inner guidance system. It may require a change of life direction, but the truth will always make you feel lighter.

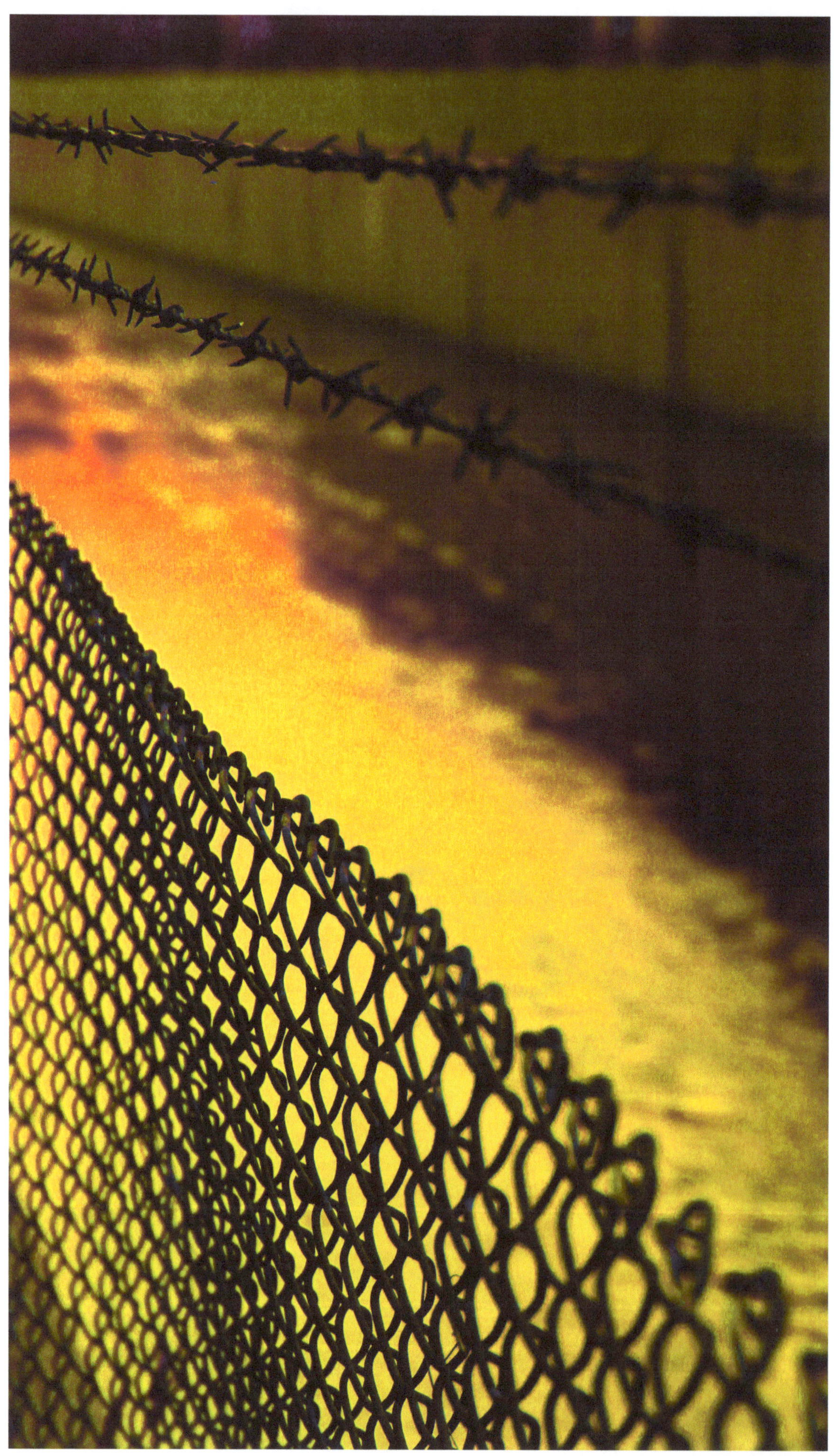

Obstacles

and challenges,

seemingly in our way,

present great lessons,

opportunities,

and prospects

for change and growth.

Discover

your divine essence.

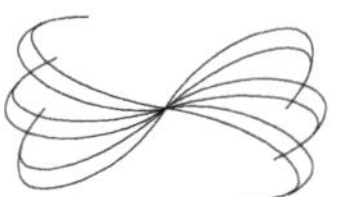

Meditation: Fear is one of your greatest obstacles and a powerful learning tool. It is also something embedded in your mind based on your past. Observe your fear, allowing yourself to feel where it is coming from. In that moment, stay with the feelings of the emotion. This is part of the healing process. As you take yourself to this place, be with the depth of your emotions. Remember emotions are "**e**nergy in **motion**." Flow the feeling and make a conscious choice to allow for progression, growth and healing.

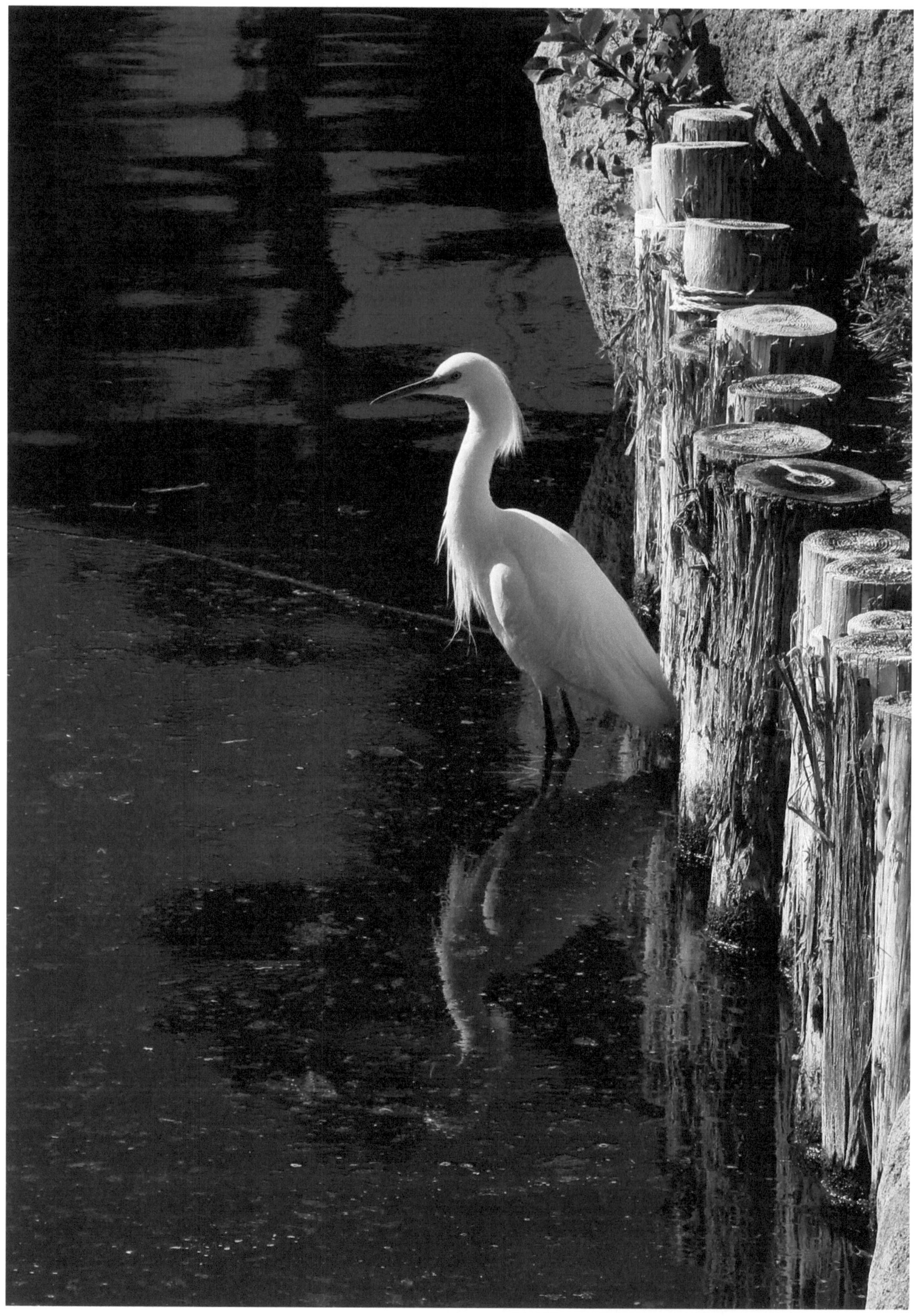

Standing on my own,

confident,

strong,

happy,

peaceful

in my solitude.

Loving myself,

knowing all is well.

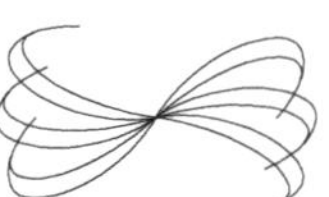

Meditation: Sit and meditate in a public place. It can be challenging, but it will further your meditation practice. No matter how chaotic the environment may be, allow yourself to be present with the surrounding elements. Let go of all thought. You can do this with your eyes open or closed. Just BE in the moment, fully present. This is a wonderful practice to help you learn to center yourself amidst the chaos of everyday life experiences.

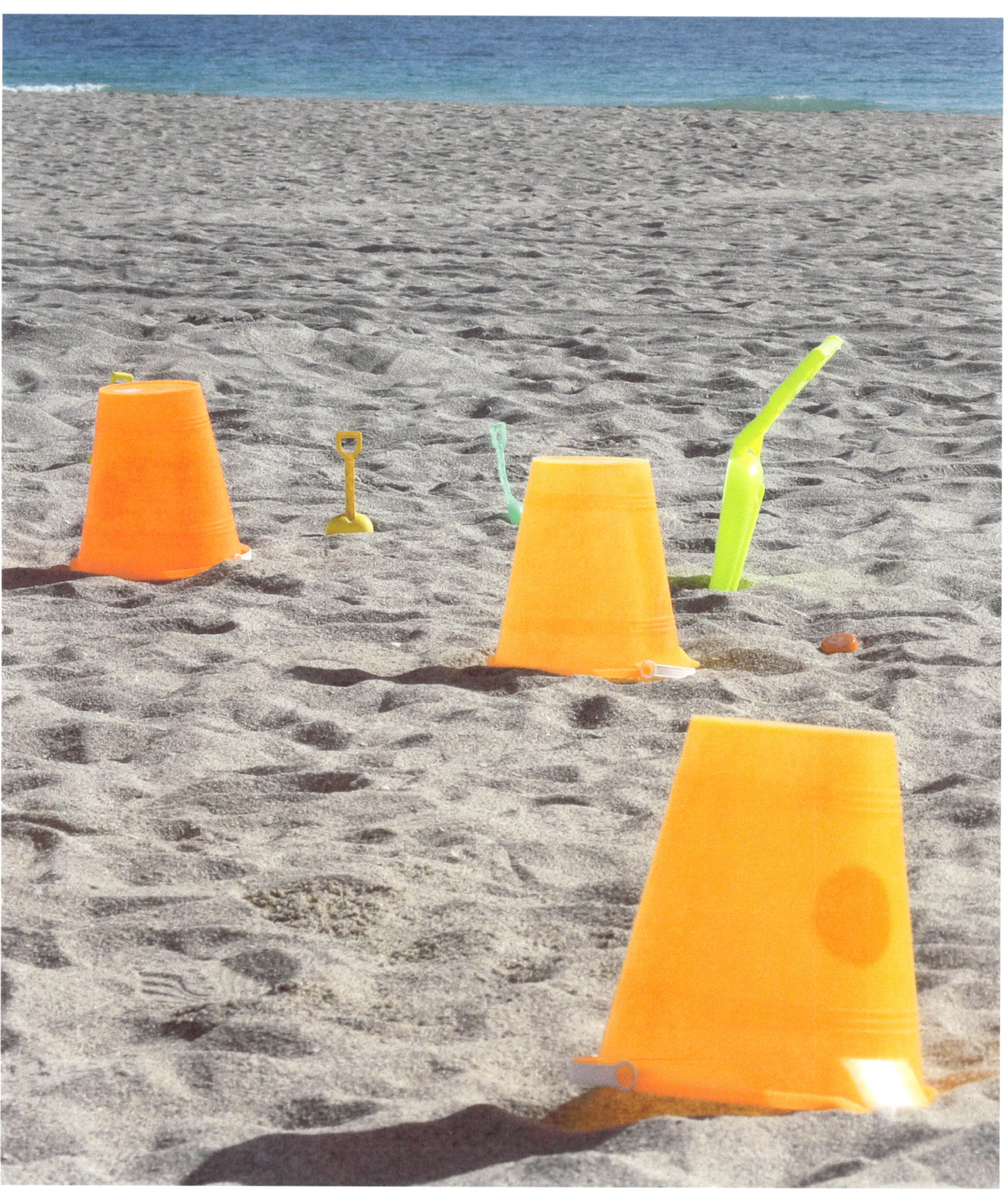

The inner child longs to play

in awe and wonder.

Exploring the universe,

dancing in spirit,

singing praises,

and dreaming in castles.

Be a kid again

in laughter and play.

Burst forth in joy and happiness.

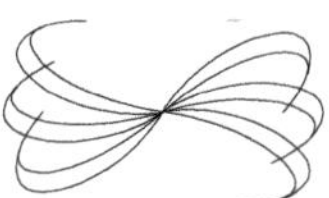

Meditation: Your inner child is your higher Self, your emotional core. It is the personality that shares your body and responds (or reacts) to situations before your adult self even has a chance to think about them. It is important to honor, love and respect your inner child by making time to play and dream. Go within and imagine yourself in a place where you can play, sing, dance and be true to your heart. This is a place where anything is possible, where you can wave a magic wand and feel safe and heard. Feel negative emotions and other obstacles melt away. You are now free to follow your heart's passions and desires. Ask your inner child what he or she wants to do today and honor that.

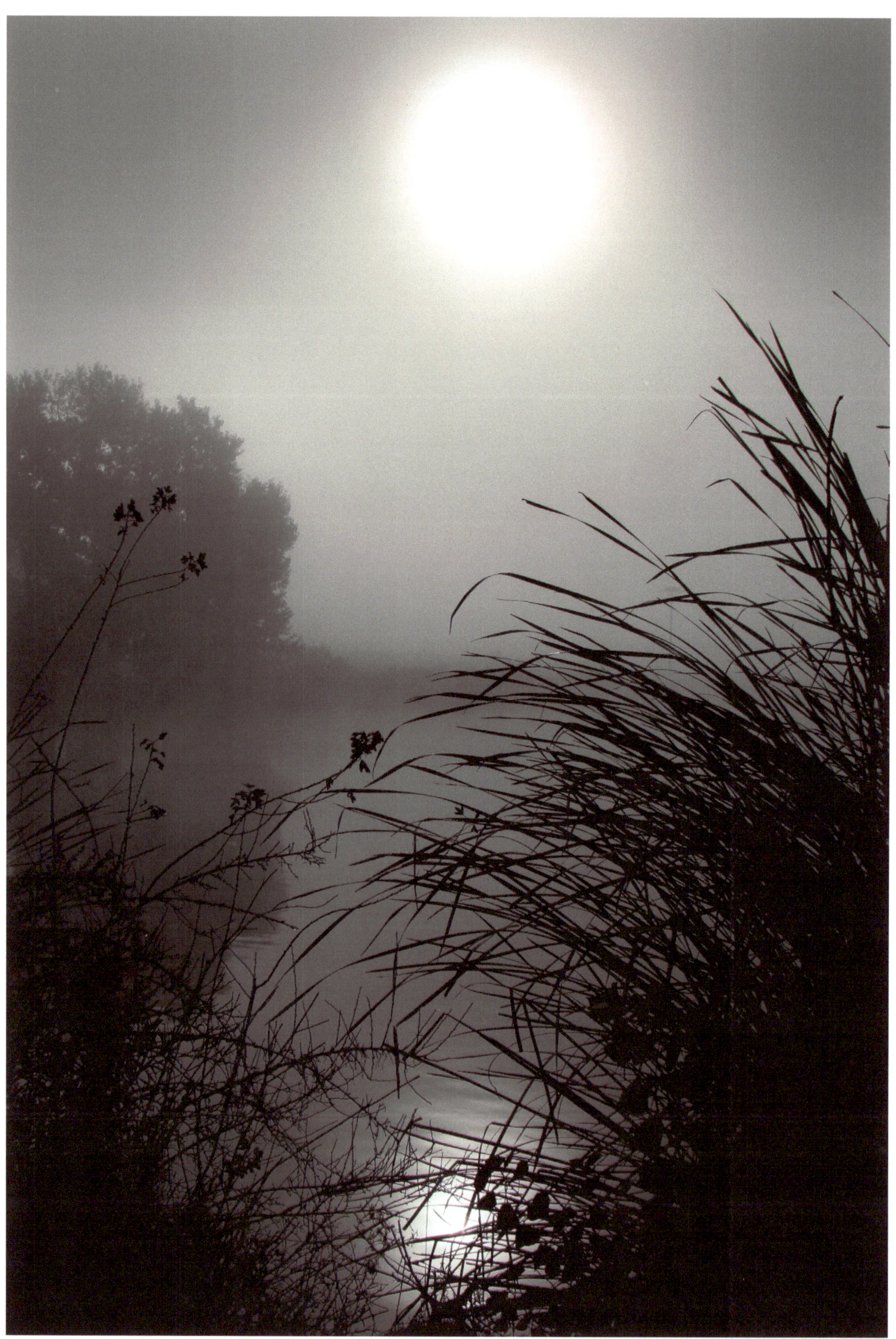

The beauty of the mysterious,

willingness to venture into the unknown.

Infinite possibilities await

if you surrender

to anticipation.

Feel the excitement building,

allowing the magic of the story to unfold.

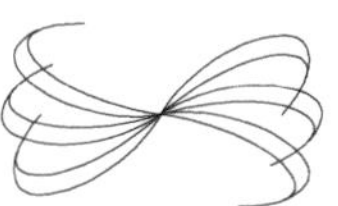

Meditation: When you open yourself to infinite possibilities, you can receive all the wonderful mysteries life offers. There is magic in the mystery of the unknown. Today, allow yourself to go within while remembering that freedom comes from detachment—there is no "right way" to look at anything in your life. Ask yourself this question: "What do I want?" Be patient as you wait and listen for your heart to speak its desires. Acknowledge them, but let go of any need to control how they will manifest. Continuing to say, "I give myself permission to let go and allow things to unfold in divine perfection."

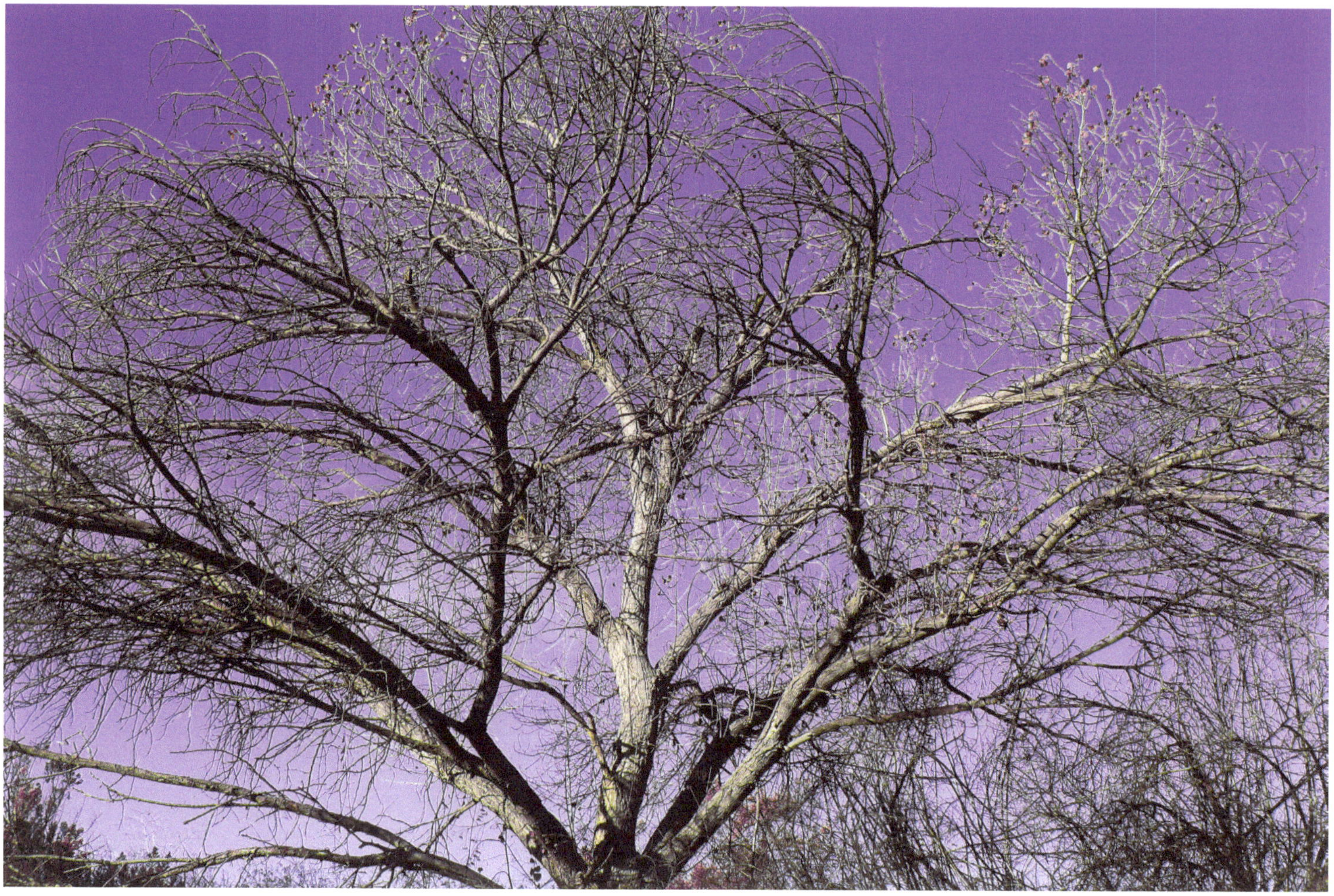

Embrace change

moment by moment,

season by season,

from one lifetime to the next.

Grant us freedom

to greet each blessing

with love and appreciation.

Savor the cycles of life.

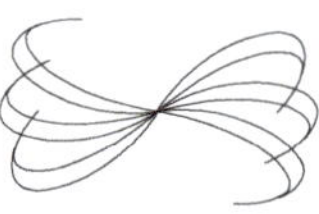

Meditation: Change is inevitable. As days, weeks and years pass, you will experience numerous changes. Set the intention to allow change to happen without resistance. Notice the emotions this intention draws to the surface. Feel them, accept them and embrace them. With each change, life presents you with the opportunity to grow. At the beginning of each day, spend some time alone and honor all that you are and all you will become. This will bring greater awareness of the beautiful cycles of change in your life.

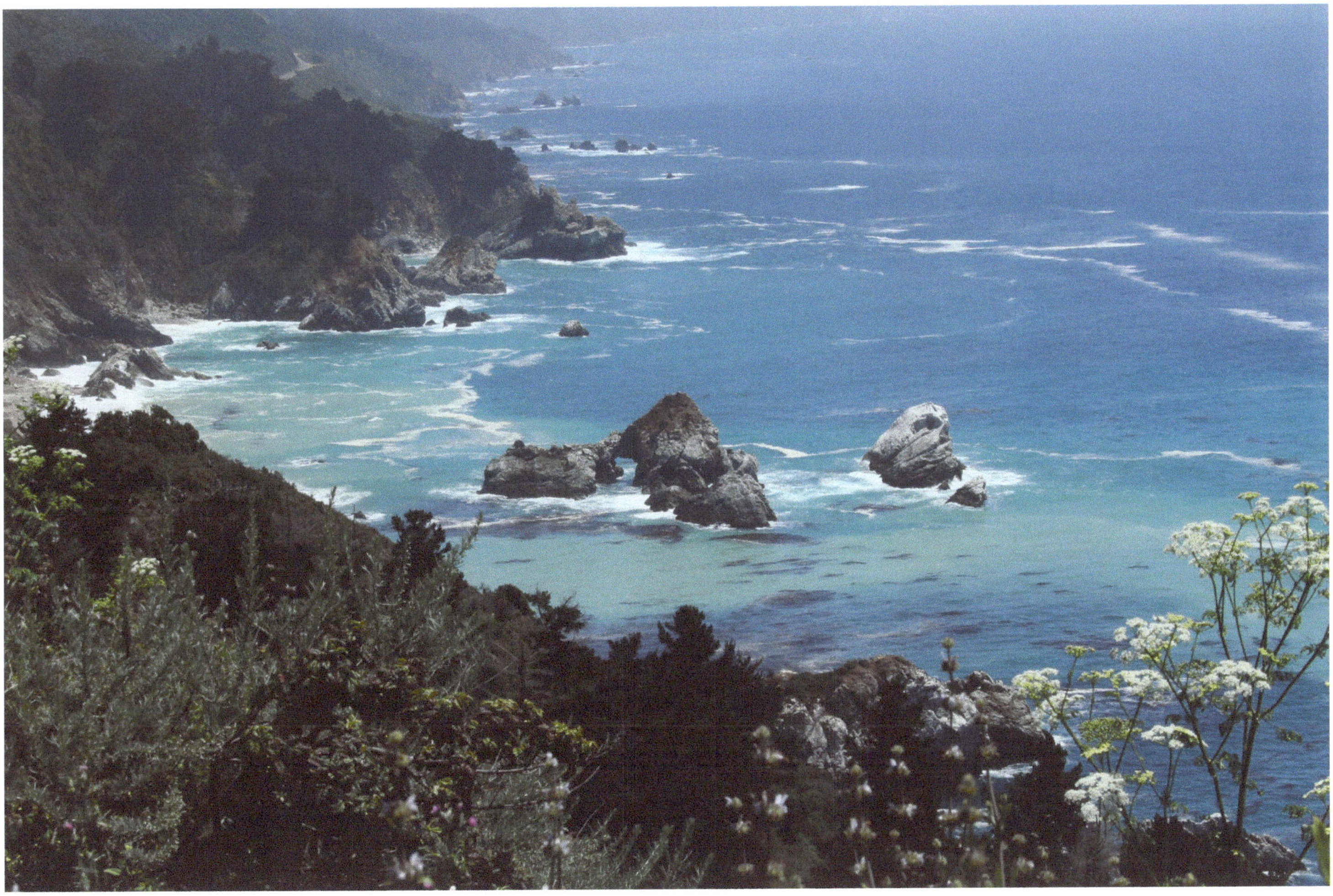

Morning coastal mist ,
lifting ,
clearing,
inspiring beauty.
Rich hues of aqua and deep blue,
rock formations rising,
waves crashing,
kissing the shoreline.
Tantalizing vision.

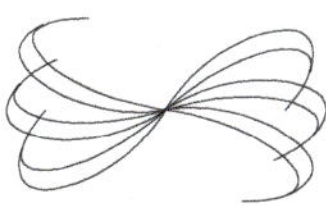

Meditation: Beauty is a gift from our Creator to help us open our hearts to the natural splendor and joys of living. Nature is breathtaking and offers us the opportunity in every moment to be awe-inspired. Take today to connect with the beauty surrounding you. Revel in the external experience and move it internally to the beauty that exists within you.

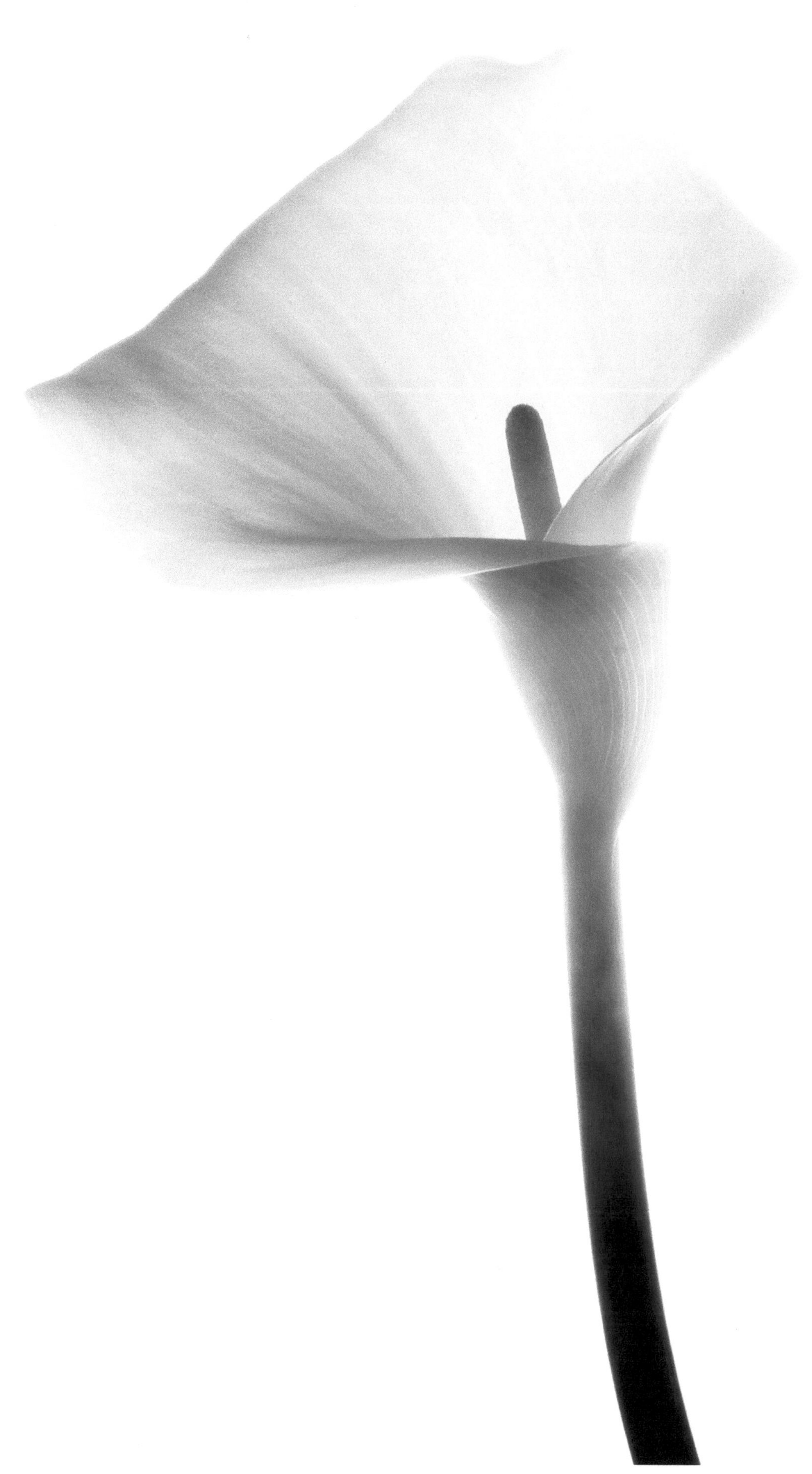

Elegance and grace

symbolizing nature's form

and beauty.

A muse of the artist.

A gift to behold.

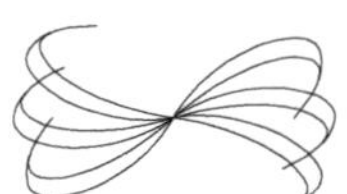

Meditation: Honoring silence is an essential healing practice. It helps us move into our heart space and connect more deeply with ourselves and others. It is in silence we can own our fears and allow ourselves to heal through pure consciousness. Today and everyday, love yourself by allowing for silent time in the morning and before going to sleep.

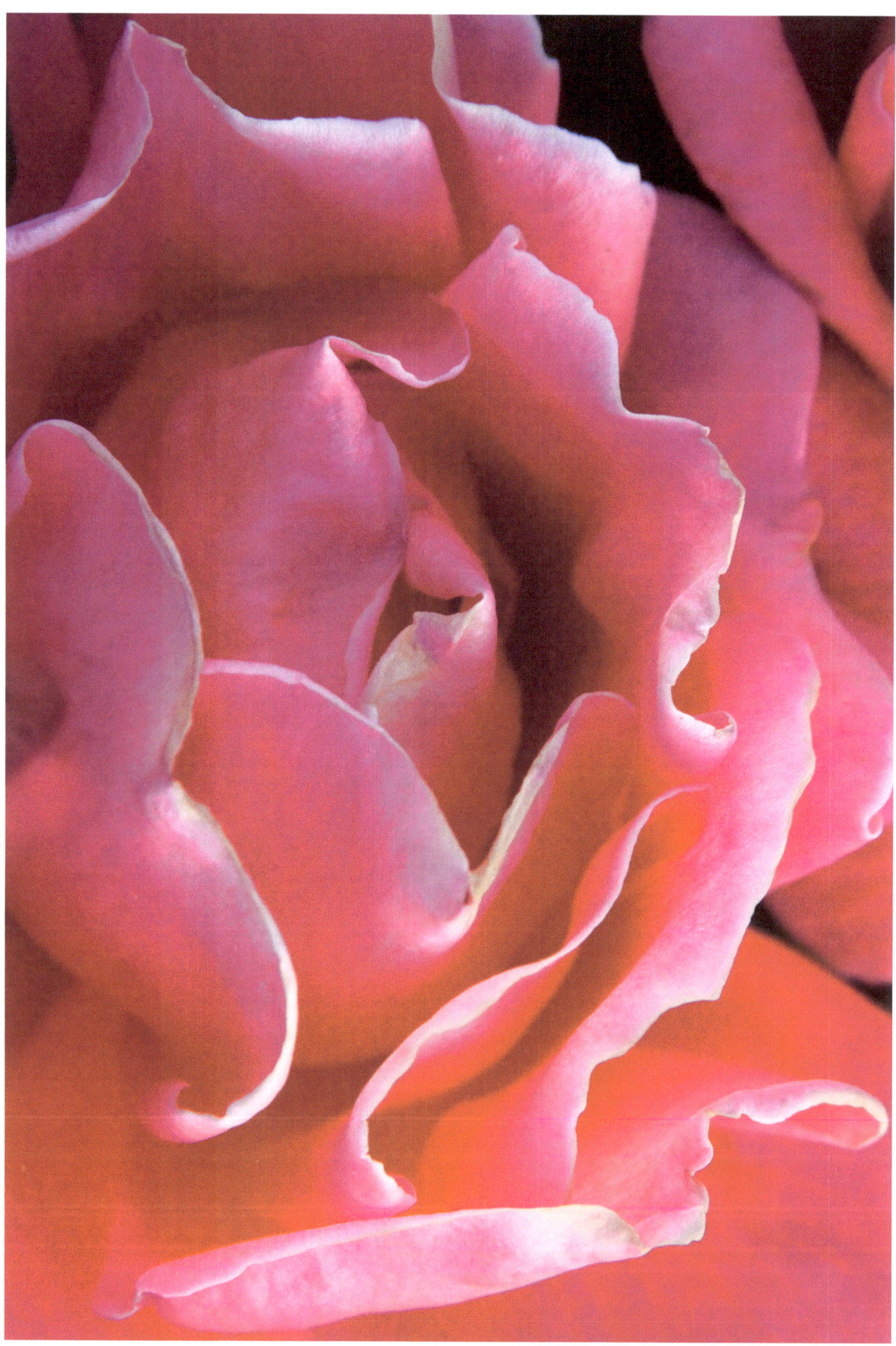

A timeless symbol of love...

Honor,

faith,

beauty,

passion,

mystique,

exquisite,

aromatic,

sensual,

A perfect rose.

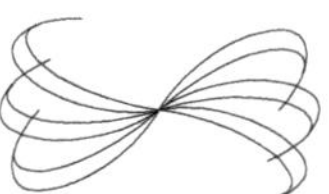

Meditation: Take a moment to check in with yourself. Are you choosing love or fear? As the Talmud states, "We do not see things as they are, we see things as we are." A simple shift in our perception can have a profound result in our lives. Ask yourself if it might be possible to see something or someone in a different way. There are multiple ways of seeing. Begin to notice how you are the creator of your own intepretive perceptions.

For more great items available and special offers from

Jeffrey Ringer Photography

visit the following link:

www.JeffreyRingerPhotography.com/BookSpecial

All Photographs in the book and more are available as printed photos, prints on canvas and printed on paper.

All photos are signed and come with a Certificate of Authenticity with a contemplative message signed by Jeffrey Ringer

For a free guided meditation from Jeffrey Ringer, go to the following link:
www.TheSpiritualHighway.com/freemeditation

Get Social with Jeffrey Ringer Photography and The Spiritual Highway

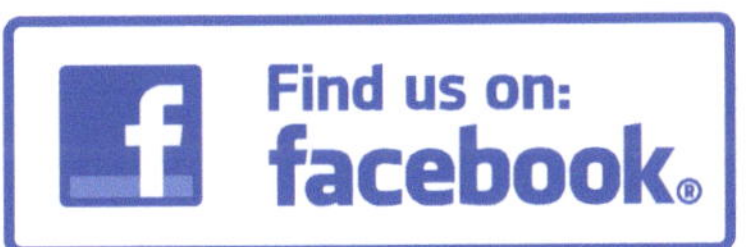

For spiritual coaching and emotional healing sessions:
www.AbundantWiseLiving.com

In Southern California and for upcoming retreats and workshops around the world, please visit:

www.TheSpiritualHighway.com
and
www.AbundantWiseLiving.com

www.ingramcontent.com/pod-product-compliance
Lightning Source LLC
LaVergne TN
LVHW071631100826
845154LV00007BA/128
* 9 7 8 0 9 9 1 0 7 9 3 0 8 *